D1576842

MEADOWS

A HISTORY AND NATURAL HISTORY

Corn poppy and white campion, *Silene alba*, make good companions in this flourishing meadow

MEADOWS

A HISTORY AND NATURAL HISTORY

JOHN FELTWELL

FOREWORD BY DR MIRIAM ROTHSCHILD

ALAN SUTTON

First published in the United Kingdom in 1992
Alan Sutton Publishing · Phoenix Mill · Far Thrupp · Stroud · Gloucestershire

First published in the United States of America in 1992
Alan Sutton Publishing Inc. · Wolfeboro Falls · NH 03896–0848

British Library Cataloguing in Publication Data

Feltwell, John, *1948–*
Meadows.
I. Title
574.526430941

ISBN 0-86299-901-4

Library of Congress Cataloging in Publication Data applied for

Typeset in 12/15 Bembo.
Typesetting and origination by
Alan Sutton Publishing Limited.
Printed and bound in Great Britain by
Hartnolls Ltd, Bodmin, Cornwall

To

Thomas Feltwell the 33rd who carries the meadow-derived name of Feltwell from the fenland village of Feltwell, from his father, John Feltwell the 40th.

Waysides burgeon with ox-eye daisy, *Leucanthemum vulgare*, docks and buttercups

CONTENTS

The ordinary daisy, *Bellis perennis*, can make a natural monocultural display, as here in an abandoned water meadow in Hérault, southern France

LIST OF ILLUSTRATIONS

Colour plates

Black and white   page

FOREWORD
by Dr Miriam Rothschild

'To see the meadows so divinely lye . . .' wrote John Clare, who was a great poet of little things. Hayfields with their buttercups and daisies are the most English expression of our country and we should treasure them and not stand by indifferently while modern farm machinery turns them into dreary mini-cornbelts.

John Feltwell's book is extremely timely for he brings home to us what we are losing by our negative acceptance of destruction that may seem an inevitable fact of modern life.

He translates dismay into figures, in other words: since the 1930s we have lost 97 per cent of our meadows – 3 per cent only remain. The smell of new-mown hay has already become a mystery, to be found only in literature, for the meadows with their sweet vernal grass and scented flowers are gone and a mono-crop of heavily fertilized Italian rye-grass provides our animal fodder. Sad.

The author describes water meadows, spring and summer pastures, downs and dunes, cornfields – which are hardly meadows but which used to contain a wonderful array of 'idle weeds' before wholesale chemical sprays destroyed them – and also alpine meadows.

As an owner of a small alpine meadow, I am delighted he has drawn attention to the catastrophic effect of massive tourism in the Alps. A small public footpath runs along the edge of my meadow and despite notices and appeals in several languages the orchids and gentians have been swept away – for considerable distance on either side of the path – by ruthless 'pickers'. Each year there are less of them – withdrawing like an ebb tide down the hillside.

The author presents timely suggestions on how to re-create flowering hayfields. Perhaps we are not too late to enjoy some really good imitation medieval meadows. For instance, it is not difficult to coax cowslips back to road verges and hayfields. Everyone interested in the English countryside should read this book and, armed with the information it contains, generate a public outcry and support John Feltwell's plea for the conservation of the pathetically few flowering meadows which are still left.

The Royal Society for Nature Conservation has succeeded in raising awareness of the plight of meadows. Let us re-establish our field flowers and then perhaps we can still hope to put the clock forward and once again be able to say:

> . . . Cuckoo buds of yellow hue
> Do paint the meadows with delight.

Miriam Rothschild

ACKNOWLEDGEMENTS

This book seems to have been a long time coming but a number of people have been very good with their time and effort. I am very grateful to Gina Douglas, Librarian of the Linnean Society in London for pursuing requests, and the Botany Library of The British Museum for use of their facilities.

Individuals who have helped with further information, assistance, guidance, opinion and reading drafts have been my wife, Carol, and Elsie Feltwell in Sussex, Lee Ann Feltwell in Philadelphia, Mary Helen Ray in Savannah, Georgia, Professor J.P. Grime of the Unit of Comparative Plant Ecology at the University of Leicester's Animal and Plant Sciences, Dr Jacques and Denise Lhonoré of the University of Maine, France, Dr Roger Smith of the Department of Agricultural and Environmental Science at the University of Newcastle upon Tyne, Donald MacIntyre of Emorsgate Seeds, Dr –Ing Günther Rauh of Munich, Dr Miriam Rothschild of Ashton Wold Wild Flowers, Bob Scott of the Royal Society for the Protection of Birds, Dr Paul Waring of the Joint Nature Conservation Committee, and Sarah Caffyn at Wildlife Matters for picture research. I would also like to give special thanks to Dr Anthea Brian of The Herefordshire Nature Trust Ltd for allowing publication of her original research on Lammas meadows as shown in tables 2.1 and 2.3.

I would like to record my thanks to the policy unit of English Nature, Peterborough, for checking certain remarks in the book, particularly grassland specialist Dr John Hopkins; to Alan Sutton Publishing, of Stroud, for permission to quote from Barclay Wills' *The Downland Shepherds,* (Beningfield *et al*, 1989); to the Royal Society for Nature Conservation for permission to quote extensively from *Losing Ground, Vanishing Meadows* (1991); to Macmillan, London, for permission to quote from *Macmillan's Guide to Nature Reserves* (1984); to Thomas Nelson and Sons Ltd, London, for permission to quote from Richard Jefferies' *Wild Life in a Southern County;* to The Regents of the University of California

Press for permission to quote passages taken from Victoria Padilla's, *Southern California Gardens, An Illustrated History,* and also for permission to quote from Christopher Thacker's 1979 *History of Gardens;* to London Editions for permission to quote United Kingdom copyright material of the previous publication; to Michael Joseph for permission to quote from Vita Sackville-West's *Garden Book;* to Penguin Books Ltd for permission to quote from both Flora Thompson's *Lark Rise to Candleford,* and Russell Page's *Education of a Gardener;* to Faber and Faber for permission to quote from Audrey Le Lièvre's *Miss Willmott of Warley Place*; and to Cambridge University Committee of Archaeology for permission to quote from the Botanical Society of the British Isles' *Archaeology and the Flora of the British Isles.* While every effort has been made to trace quoted material this has not always been possible. Any omissions will be rectified in future reprints.

As for illustrations, I would like to express my thanks to Mrs Holden of the Museum of Rural Life at Reading University for guiding me through their one million-strong archive of historic prints and for permission to reproduce plates 35, 48, 67, 69, 70, 82, 84, 94, 105; The Mary Evans Picture Library for plates 49, 66, 118; and Giraudon/The Bridgeman Art Library for plate 4. I am very grateful to the National Wildflower Research Center in Austin, Texas, for permission to reproduce Laura Barton's photograph, plate 96, of Mrs Lyndon Johnson in a wild flower meadow, and to Mrs Lyndon Johnson herself for permission to reproduce plates 98, 106, 115 (via her agent in Britain, Dr Miriam Rothschild); to Dr Miriam Rothschild for permission to use plate 60; to The Mansell Collection for permission to reproduce plate 36; to the Roquefort Société in France for permission to use plate 85; to The Royal Society for Nature Conservation for the use of Carol Roberts' black and white illustrations, plates 38, 40, 116; to Heather Angel/RSNC for permission to use the portrait of HRH Prince Charles, plate 64; to Sarah Anne Hughes/World Conservation Monitoring Centre, Cambridge, for permission to use plate 103. I am particularly indebted to Valerie Baines, FLS, ARMS for her two pieces of original colour artwork.

Finally I would like to express my thanks to the editorial team at Alan Sutton Publishing, particularly Peter Clifford and Jaqueline Mitchell, for smoothly guiding this book through to publication.

LATIN NAMES

In order that the text is relatively uncluttered with Latin names, those of important species have been placed in tables for clarification. The Latin names for those in Europe are in accordance with those published in Dony *et al* (1986), Polunin (1981) and Clapham *et al* (1962). Those in North America follow *Hortus Third* (1976).

Early-purple orchids, *Orchis mascula*, growing in an ancient meadow at Marden in Kent, now a nature reserve managed by the Kent Trust for Nature Conservation

INTRODUCTION

And did those feet in ancient time
Walk upon England's mountains green?
And was the holy Lamb of God
On England's pleasant pastures seen?

William Blake, 'Jerusalem'

This book is written almost too late. The best meadows have gone, the cornucopia of meadowland has disappeared and the choice of heavenly examples is in massive decline. The problems of meadows are international, and directly correlate with man's pressure on land. Some would blame global warming as well. In Britain, at least, there are only 3 per cent of meadows left. The 97 per cent of meadows which disappeared in the last sixty years took a thousand or so years to evolve. What has disappeared before our eyes is frustratingly difficult to re-create.

But meadows are a product of man's use of the land, and without man there would have been few meadows, certainly no lowland meadows. Like hedgerows, meadows are man-made, or at least man-managed, and their demise should be put in this context. If man had not taken hay from meadows, or grazed the land, there would be no meadows, simply woodland and forest. There would always have been light woodlands studded with carpets of flowers in the spring, and clearings of wild flowers, as well as open heathland and fresh alluvial land beside large rivers which would have had their own meadows, but the majority of meadows as we know them today have been fashioned by the hand of man and by his beasts.

It is quite likely that many of the documented ancient meadows of England are in fact over two thousand years old, one thousand years older than previously believed. It would appear from evidence that when man first learned to cut with an iron scythe, the first of the ancient meadows started to diversify in England, particularly along the alluvial plain of the river Thames. Since evidence of implements used for cutting hay does not exist before the Iron Age, it is tempting to think that ancient meadows may be older than two thousand years. Despite this tantalizing realization of meadow longevity, many of the terms for haymaking are in fact of more recent, Saxon origin. So this is food for thought when one contemplates that 97 per cent of the ancient meadows of Britain have so far been destroyed. What remains, the 3 per cent, is very precious.

There will never be a return to the rolling countryside full of rich meadows that Chesterton typical of the end of the last century; and a journey along a favourite river valley will never be as it was a hundred years ago, with lush water meadows, glebe fields and rich pastures on either side. That time has gone. For ever.

Since the history of meadows is ancient, it is hardly surprising that it has permeated society to such a degree that it has shaped the way villages are constructed, how and where villagers and their animals are deployed in the fields, and above all, pervaded English literature. There is probably no other country which has such a meadow heritage locked up in its way of life.

Fortunately, those invigorating scenes were captured by ordinary men and women who wrote about the rosy countryside they saw, and which simply stimulated them. Even in comparatively recent times, at the turn of the century, Edith Holden wrote of July days in Warwickshire full of delightful water meadows, clouds of meadow brown butterflies and 'sedgy' streams. Her revelations later gained the sympathy of a huge public, when published as *The Country Diary of an Edwardian Lady*, who perhaps realized that they were fast losing all these wondrous scenes. One only has to gaze at Helen Allingham's paintings of cottages to see the kind of lusty environment in which they sat, looking over marvellous water meadows, acres of colourful flowers and, as always, clouds of butterflies. The joy was shared even as recently as 1945 when Flora Thompson recalled her turn of the century childhood in *Lark Rise to Candleford*. After the 1950s, however, there was a profound change, and something went very wrong for meadows.

In one sense *Meadows* is about village life, about the lives of these ordinary people who came and went from the meadows and pastures that

The Church in England often owned meadows in the parish, frequently close to the village or town centre, as here near Worcester Cathedral where haymakers load their crop within a few hundred metres of the city centre. Church-owned meadows were called 'glebe' lands

surrounded their communities. And about the food they ate, the way it tasted, the way it smelt, and of fresh hay cut and stooked. And it is about the sights and sounds of the English village, about Lammas meadows, teart meadows, lags and pingoes. It is also about the church, and about its glebe meadows which helped to shape each village – in a way that is uniquely English, since no other country has this sort of history woven round its meadows. On the continent the pressure on the countryside is considerably less than in Britain, and wild flowers and butterflies are sometimes still seen in great abundance. There, enjoying species that can only now be found in England in text books, it is like taking a trip to good ol' England as she used to be, or as we imagine she used to be. The floristic abundance of France was recognized at least in the seventeenth century by George Herbert (1640), who wrote, *'France est un pré qui se fond trois foys l'années'* (France is a meadow that cuts thrice a year).

There is a meadow heritage in North America but it is an awfully recent one. Place names help us to picture the original habitat – Star Prairie, Meadowbrook, Prairie City, even Flushing Meadow – and we can imagine the pioneer settlers pushing onward through thousands of acres of colourful carpets of flowers, not really appreciating the wealth of botanical diversity under their feet.

The spectacular wilderness in North America, with its sheets of seasonal meadow, was appreciated by such outdoor men as the famous John Muir, who eventually saved precious parts of the High Sierras for the nation by canvassing and motivating politicians. And by the less well-known Aldo Leopold, who started the initiatives at countryside stewardship and wilderness preservation in the southern states of Arizona and New Mexico in the 1920s.

It is not just wilderness which is under threat in the USA. Ordinary agricultural land and meadows are being swallowed up at an alarming rate. The facts speak for themselves. Since the Second World War about 28–40 million hectares of open space have been lost. In just one state – New Jersey – 9,720 hectares of farmland were lost each year between 1950 and 1986, and this then jumped to 19,000 hectares in the following two years (Davis, T., 1991).

The only sad aspect about this retrospective look at meadows is that we shall never see them in all their glory as was commonplace for Shakespeare, Wordsworth or Milton. It all has to be savoured as fond memories, and read about in our precious literature. Several of the important meadow plants and animals are also now so rare that few ever have a chance to see them in the wild, whether they be corncockles or corncrakes. I have had to write about some meadow plants, insects and birds which I have never seen, which are part of our heritage, but are never seen. This is not new. J.E. Lousley, the British expert on chalk-loving plants, said in his 1950s book that he had never seen the lady's-slipper orchid in the wild, it being one of the rarest and most elusive of British plants. And the gifted lexicographer of English plants, Geoffrey Grigson, said in 1958 that he had never seen the corncockle in Wiltshire where once it thrived. We, on the other hand, can have corncockle in our own backyard thanks to the wildflower seed boom.

All is not gloom and doom however. This book is definitely not about the catastrophic demise of our missing meadows: that cataloguing is done regularly by conservation organizations – whose results can be looked up. Neither is this book just about the 3 per cent of meadows left in Britain, with their key meadow species, such as yellow rattle, common sorrel, quaking-grass and ox-eye daisy. The book is retrospective for the sheer joy of unravelling the history of meadows, and future-looking, since there *is* an upsurge in interest in re-creating meadows. A positive approach is taken to meadows throughout this book, leaving aside the minutiae of the negative aspects of their demise, and meadows both in the New and Old Worlds are considered.

So what is the difference between meadows and pastures? Some meadows can actually be pastures as well as meadows, and a confusing 'meadow-pasture' is known in places. But normally there is a relatively clear distinction between meadows which were cut for hay, and pastures which were grazed by stock. Meadows were often referred to as being 'up for hay', suggesting that walking through the standing hay crop was to be discouraged. In fact, this difference in management expresses itself in the plants present. In pastures there is a greater incidence of plants which have leaves in the form of rosettes on the surface of the ground, such as daisies, plantains, cat's-ears and dandelions, as well as thistles and ragwort, than in hay meadows, which are made up of plants which have long stems. So botanically the difference is as fundamental as that: low-growing and tall-growing plants. Of course, if grazers are removed, then low-growing plants slowly disappear in favour of tall-growing plants. Both meadows and pastures are different types of grassland.

Certain plants and animals are commonly taken as indicators of healthy environments, including meadows. As well as describing the wild plants, a discussion of butterflies has been incorporated within the text of this book because they are also becoming important visual indicators of healthy habitats, especially meadows.

The need to protect what is remaining of all our semi-natural or natural habitats increases as human populations increase. Demands on the countryside continue unabated, whether it is patchwork England with its meadows and pastures, North American wilderness, or numerous parts of Europe where meadows survive between alien environments devoid of any plant life.

The countryside – including its rich meadows – is in danger of being gobbled-up completely by man and his development, and the Germans

In this fifteenth-century Flemish scene, men and women are cutting the hay, using straight-handled scythes, gathering it up into small stacks and hauling it away on carts. There is the customary refreshment at hand for such hard work. The meadow seems to be bright with meadow flowers

have an apposite way of putting this – the '*Landschaftsfresser*', which means quite simply the 'landscape-eater'. Man is certainly culpable. Contrasting with the *Landschaftsfresser* is the positive aspect to our diminishing habitats, *Ruhezonen* – or areas which should be left undisturbed by man.

The greatest impact of man on meadows can be summed up in one word: improvement. This seemingly-pleasant term, couched in such splendid innuendo, might sway the novice into thinking that meadows are actually improved. The 'improvement' is entirely one-sided, that of the farmers. Acting in simple good faith to earn a living from the soil, the farmer frequently drains the land in order to grow new crops. Spraying weed-killers and drainage are about the worst procedures, except for grubbing out and ploughing, which damage meadows or pasture.

The effects of global warming on British flora are currently being investigated by various research establishments in Britain. One of these, at the University of Sheffield led by Professor J.P. Grime, is studying in the laboratory the effects of warming and cooling on the performance of various native plants. Under particular scrutiny are a number of species found in the north or in the south of their range in Britain. The northerly ones like it cool, and will therefore, presumably not like it warming up, and, in reverse, the southern species might enjoy warmer conditions and expand northwards. The following table (from NERC, 1990, pp. 431 and 433) lists those species which may be in the news a little longer as global warming continues.

More abundant in north species

Burnet, great	*Sanguisorba officinalis*
Buttercup, meadow	*Ranunculus acris*
Crane's-bill, wood	*Geranium sylvaticum*
Globeflower	*Trollius europaeus*
Meadow-grass, rough	*Poa trivialis*
Pignut	*Conopodium majus*
Sorrel, common	*Rumex acetosa*

More abundant in south species

Clover, red	*Trifolium pratense*
Dog's-tail, crested	*Cynosurus cristatus*
Fritillary, snake's-head	*Fritillaria meleagris*
Saxifrage, pepper	*Silaum silaus*

One of the intentions of this research is to find ways of re-creating meadows and restoring some of the more esoteric meadow flowers to the countryside. Work carried out in 1991 by Sue Hillier has been with the snake's-head fritillary and the meadow crane's-bill, both species which are in great need of being reinstated into the British countryside.

Many of us have seen the decline of our native flora, and it is understandable that we want it all back, at least in our own backyards. We probably all know of some wild flower which within our own lifetime used to be common. This enthusiasm for wild flower seeds and meadow mixes, even 'meadows in a can' on the supermarket shelves of California, has produced a new word for the English language. Not just plain old 'wild flowers', it has been upstaged to a single word – 'wildflowers'. And it has spilled over into our gardens.

Perhaps this enthusiasm for meadows goes deeper, to the need in all of us to re-create those lovely meadows of our childhood, to bring together all those colourful wild flowers of the countryside. Wildflower gardening has become the epitome of meadow reinstatement. The enthusiasm with which ordinary people buy packets of wildflower seed, seems to suggest that perhaps we are all crying out for that extra amount of jazzy colour in our lives. After all, the countryside is very colourful when in full bloom.

The essence of gardening *per se* is really an interpretation of the pleasures of the countryside, of the floral delights of waysides and woodland, encapsulated and expressed in the garden milieu. And it is always a very personal experience, between man and nature. Yet, perhaps gardening with wildflowers goes much deeper than this, philosophically. Perhaps the wildflower garden is the 'pleasure garden' of yesterday, a place to enjoy, to be at peace with oneself – the 'pleasance' of ancient Greece. As Ruskin wrote, 'The best image which the world can give of Paradise is in the slope of the meadows, orchards and cornfields on the sides of a great Alp.'

The origins of meadow gardening are in fact the same as those of gardening itself. Christopher Thacker traces the origin of gardens in his classic book, *The History of Gardens*, and treats us to many early examples of gardens in the Old World with meadows in them. It is perhaps not surprising that the earliest 'pleasure gardens' are ones which incorporate an element of 'meadow'. Although this is clear in reading Thacker's book, it is not a point to which he draws attention. The first flower gardens simply re-created the colourful meadows of the countryside. They were the first

Donald MacIntyre of Emorsgate Seeds grows hectares of wildflowers such as this familiar yarrow, *Achillea millefolium*, on the rich alluvial soil of Norfolk. Like lady's bedstraw, yarrow has an overpowering scent when grown *en masse*

manifestations of gardening for aesthetic considerations, rather than for practical purposes such as growing fruit and vegetables in a kitchen garden.

In ancient Greece and Rome, the countryside was allowed to come right into the garden. An inanimate expression of the joys of the countryside was also incorporated into the garden plan. Empress Livia's garden in Rome has the murals of birds and plants depicted on its walls, as if to keep a permanent reminder of the close connection between the garden and the outside world. Water was also an important element in the garden, especially in the ancient Persian, Moorish and Spanish gardens, and this attracted many birds.

As Thacker explains, the pleasure garden in ancient Rome, based on a combination of the fact and fiction regarding the vale of Temple, was the:

> quintessential *locus amoenus*, the 'pleasant place', the unspoilt, intended meadow or glade of classical and medieval times. . . . Commonly, the medieval garden of pleasure, whether knightly or spiritual, will centre round a 'flowery mede', a space of meadow-grass sprinkled with innumerable flowers, where Adam and Eve, Virgin and Child, knights and ladies will gather for moments of recreation and delight.

Early in the sixteenth century the Mughal gardens in India and modern Afghanistan were rich in meadows. They were the result of the gardening enthusiasm of the Emperor Babur (1483–1530) and descriptions and illustrations of these remain. One near Jalalabad is depicted as a trefoil meadow encircling a garden containing orange trees, pomegranates, bananas and sugar cane. Apparently the garden was a most beautiful sight when the oranges took colour, when they presumably colour-matched the deep yellow/orange of the trefoil. The Italians during the Renaissance liked to stroll through the wooded and flowery countryside, and Henry VIII had his banqueting halls built among glades of the forest, as at Nonesuch Park with its petrified griffons.

Modern man feels an affinity with meadows, their flowering freedom, the random arrangement of grasses and the profusion of colourful flowers. It is an image which permeates modern life in so many artificial ways, such as in advertising and decor. The meadow holds a fascination for us all and this book aims to help us to know and to understand its enchantment.

CHAPTER 1

CORNFIELDS

The pink pimpernel hides on the very verges of the corn, which presently will be strewn with the beautiful 'bluebottle' flower, than whose exquisite hue there is nothing more lovely in our fields.

Richard Jefferies, from *Wild Life in a Southern County*, p. 59

Traditionally, a typical field of corn was a kaleidoscope of colour, a natural mixture of wild flowers which thrived in man's turned soil. Now the situation has changed, and the colourful fields of corn are losing their gay variety of flowers and are taking on a uniform golden hue – which is just what the farmer wants. Occasionally on less intensely-worked land the wild flowers pop back, most notably the corn poppy.

Today, in Europe many of the beautiful countryside scenes of the past of fields full of blossom are confined to books of Impressionist paintings, by Van Gogh, Degas or Monet. Those delightful Provençal scenes, of deep blue skies, and swathes of scarlet mixed with pink, blue and white can, however, still be found in the wilder parts of southern Europe where intensification of agriculture has been slow to become the norm – where wild flower seed survives in the soil and produces another new crop of flowers among man's crops, a legacy from at least one thousand years ago.

The diversity of the wild flowers springing from the earth is much greater around the shores of the Mediterranean than in Britain for instance, and represents a much more uninterrupted habitat. Sadly, many young-sters now only get to see re-created meadows and flowery fields sown by conservationists eager to reinstate the glories of the past – and to appreciate the plants that their grandmothers used to know and talk about.

The colour of ancient cornfields then would have been inevitable, such is the power of the plants to colonize and to lie dormant in the soil. Man has always tried to grow corn[1] as a pure crop, but the appearance of his cornfields would have belied this intention. Amazingly, this is still the situation today in parts of Provence, round the fertile Camargue delta, and it would have been much more prevalent in medieval times. Time has changed very little in that region, certainly in recent times since the Impressionists produced their colourful paintings of what they saw.

These were also the days in England when waysides, downs and fields were full of mixed colour, when people were not too bothered about these weedy 'rogues' or about economic returns, even before herbicides were invented (in the 1940s). In the United States, where there are many more opportunities for plants, wild flowers are good performers and still thrive in wilderness areas. The United States has been able to maintain a much wilder stance with major centres of population on the margins and the great interior of the country free to blossom in the wilder areas originally cleared by Indians and now not so overrun by man.

Common cornfield species, left to right: scarlet pimpernel, *Anagalis arvensis*; rough poppy, *Papaver hybridum*; corncockle, *Agrostemma githago*; and field pansy, *Viola tricolor*

Table 1.1 Corn relics
(from various sources, such as Horwood (1919), Grieve, (1980))

A number of plants have as their second name *arvensis*, Latin for field, further emphasizing the cornfield habitat in which they were found, perhaps with the corn, on the margins, or growing in great abundance after the corn was gathered in.

	Old Name	**Latin Name**
Corn bellflower	Venus's-looking-glass	*Legousia speculum-veneris*
Corn bindweed	convolvulus (also cornbind, cornbine) and black bindweed	*Convolvulus arvensis* *Fallopia convolvulus*
Corn binks	cornflower	*Centaurea cyanus*
Corn bottle	cornflower	*Centaurea cyanus*
Corn buttercup		*Ranunculus arvensis*
Corn cail	charlock	*Sinapis arvensis*
Corn campion		*Silene* sp.
Corn centaury		*Centaurium* sp.
Corn chervil	shepherd's needle	*Scandix pecten-veneris*
Corncockle		*Agrostemma githago*
Corn crowfoot		*Ranunculus* sp.
Corn feverfew		*Matricaria inodora*
Cornflower or corn bottle		*Centaurea cyanus*
Corn gromwell		*Lithospermum arvense*
Corn honewort		*Trinia glauca*
Corn lily	convolvulus	*Convolvulus arvensis*
Corn marigold		*Chrysanthemum segetum*
Corn melilot, or Ribbed melilot		*Melilotus officinalis*
Corn mint		*Mentha arvensis*
Corn mustard		*Brassica* sp.
Corn parsley		*Petroselinum segetum*
Corn pink	ragged-robin (also meadow pink, or spinks)	*Lychnis flos-cuculi*
Corn pop	bladder campion	*Silene vulgaris*
Corn poppy		*Papaver rhoeas*
Corn rose	corn poppy	*Papaver rhoeas*
Cornsalad		*Valerianella locusta*
Corn sow-thistle		*Sonchus arvensis*
Corn spurrey		*Spergula arvensis*
Corn thistle		*Cirsium* sp.
Corn violet		*Viola* sp.
Corn woodruff	woodruff	*Galium odoratum*

In earliest times wherever man tilled the soil wild flowers would compete with his crops. Feeding the family was always, of course, important: stashing away stores for the winter, selling a bit of extra crop, and continually fighting weeds, disease and insects were all part of daily agricultural life. Mass production was not the aim, so a few extra weeds were not so assiduously pursued as they would be later, especially if they were colourful. But there were very serious 'rogues', such as the wild oat, which degraded grain, was less nutritious and was a real menace to eradicate. It still is. Walking through cornfields pulling or cutting wild oats or thistles was the usual form, as John Clare reminds us in *The Shepherd's Calendar*:

> Each morning now the weeders meet
> To cut the thistle from the wheat
> And ruin in the sunny hours
> Full many wild weeds of their flowers
> Corn poppies that in crimson dwell
> Call'd 'head achs' from their sickly smell.

John Clare was speaking of village life during May in the county of Northamptonshire over a hundred and twenty years ago. Wild oats and thistles were not the only pests, poppies were removed too, and this was called 'poping'. Today, all corn 'weeds' are eliminated in one sweep of the herbicide nozzle.

Tilling the soil kept the field clear for wild flowers, but so too did grazing. In southern France irrefutable evidence demonstrates that man has domesticated goats for four thousand years, for at Cambous in the Hérault *département* many old bones of goats and sheep have been found around an archaeological site which has been researched during the last decade or so.[2] In this area at least we can assume that colourful meadows existed around man's encampments, when they were not cut for bedding, hay or allowed for grazing. Man perhaps encroached upon some of the open meadow areas by the side of streams, where for thousands of years before wild animals such as deer and, to a lesser extent, wild boar maintained open pastures by rooting around.

It is interesting that the colourful meadows which we associate with the countryside are not really its natural state. Today's countryside is a product

Table 1.2   Typical corn flowers in southern Europe

Candytuft	*Iberis amara*
Corncockle	*Agrostemma githago*
Cornflower	*Centaurea cyanus*
Cornsalad, common	*Valerianella locusta*
Corn marigold	*Chrysanthemum segetum*
Heart's-ease violet	*Viola tricolor*
Knapweed, common	*Centaurea nigra*
Mallow, common	*Malva sylvestris*
Pheasant's-eye	*Adonis annua*
Pimpernel, scarlet	*Anagallis arvensis*, sub-species *arvensis*
Poppy, commonly 'corn poppy'	*Papaver rhoeas*
Venus's-looking-glass	*Legousia speculum-veneris*

of the times since man started to make inroads into the wild woods and forests which once covered most of the countryside. It is said that most of the landscape that we see today in southern England is entirely shaped by man, and that nothing is what it originally was.[3] And the patchwork fields and meadows of the countryside which are typical of the English lowlands are actually the result of the numerous Enclosure Acts of the eighteenth and nineteenth centuries. The colourful wild flowers would have been there originally in glades and along the margins of woods, waiting to exploit man's tilled soil. Flowers would have experienced dramatic embellishment and radical extensions of their ranges through the actions of man clearing the land. Their niche was secure, or at least for a while it was.

It seemed wholly fitting that we should appropriate these wild flowers of the countryside for our own pleasure gardens; after all, children in country areas pick wild flowers intuitively, as they grow up surrounded by masses of colour. Since gardening began, man has always sought to embellish the garden with wild gems, and to find flowers which had something slightly different from the norm, whether it was a four-leaved clover or an albino plant or a double flower. And so it was with the corn poppy.

The Reverend Wilks of Shirley, near Croydon, Surrey (now part of south-east London's suburbs) saw one day a corn poppy which differed in colour from the rest. He kept the seed of this plant and through progressive raising and artificially selecting for the different colours of the petals eventually produced a strain of poppy which became known as the Shirley

In 1988 the pheasant's-eye, *Adonis annua*, was adopted as the symbol of the revival of wild flowers in Britain's crops by the British Agrochemicals Association, Game Conservancy and English Nature

poppy. Such was the importance of this selection process and the popularity of the poppy that Wilks's Shirley poppy is remembered in relief in the wrought-iron gates at Wisley – the showpiece garden of The Royal Horticultural Society of which Wilks was secretary.

Thus a familiar cornfield wild flower was established in the garden in a form which is both pleasant, different and delightful; today, a packet of Shirley poppy seeds ('Shirley Single Mixed' or 'Shirley Double Mixed') produces a range of soft pastel colours, of pink, white, rose and salmon – a long way from the bright colours which decorated the Impressionists's palettes, or the flowering cornfields of the waysides.

More species of the cornfield, left to right: long-headed poppy, *Papaver dubium*; corn buttercup, *Ranunculus arvensis*; cornflower, *Centaurea cyanus*; and field forget-me-not, *Myosotis arvensis*

There is also another interesting poppy grown in gardens, and wild gardens. It is the Iceland poppy, *Papaver nudicale*, which was introduced to Britain as early as 1730 from the sub-Arctic meadows of Canada and Siberia.

But what of the flora and fauna of the typical cornfield? A hundred years ago in the English countryside there were many more birds in a cornfield than there are today in the serried ranks of the new varieties of short corn. The old varieties of corn were up to a metre high, providing ample cover for wildlife, unlike today's short corn of 0.3 metre or so high.

Many a vignette about the birds of the cornfields during the nineteenth century can be read in the meanderings of Richard Jefferies who came to live in south-east England and wrote about his observations. For instance, on skylarks:

In the early spring, when love-making is in full progress, the cornfield where the young green blades are just showing become the scene of the most amazing rivalry. Far as the eye can see across the ground it seems alive with larks – chasing each other to fro, round and round, with excited calls, flying close to the surface, continually alighting, and springing up again. . . . Some seem always to remain in the meadows; but the majority frequent the arable land, and especially the cornfields in the slopes of the downs, where they may be found in such numbers as rival or perhaps exceed those of any other bird.[4]

Perhaps one of the most historical of cornfield birds is the corncrake. It is sadly a very rare bird in Britain, and one that few have actually seen today, having been extinguished from a lot of its range and now only seen in the west of Ireland or west Scotland. But we are fortunate in having several telling accounts of the bird, which was very common in southern England when Jefferies made his observations. He speaks of the bird which has the voice of a ventriloquist, since it will 'crake–crake' and appear close-by but you are unable to locate it. Possibly the bird had a penchant for singing along the furrows cut by the plough across the field and thus was able to throw its voice more effectively. He speaks of the workers in the meadow cutting the hay and coming across corncrake eggs which are brought to 'the farmstead, both as a curiosity and to be eaten, some thinking them equal to plover's eggs.' Jefferies description of corncrakes suggest that they favour certain meadows:

The home-field or meadow here is a favourite haunt of the crakes, for, like all other birds, they have their special places of resort. Another meadow, at some distance on the same farm, is equally favoured by them . . . they appear to restrict themselves to the field they have chosen, or, at the furthest, make an excursion into the next and return again, so that you may always know where to go to hear one.[5]

There were, of course, always plenty of insects and invertebrates, such as beetles and spiders, to satisfy the appetite of such ground-dwelling birds as the corncrake, grouse, partridge and pheasant. Butterflies also cavorted among the blossoms of the 'canopy' of the corn crop and among the shorter-stemmed flowers which blossomed in the gaps in the corn. With such an abundance of corn flowers the field would have been alive with a shimmering mass of butterflies flitting from one flower to the next, or

This is a typical corncrake meadow in western Ireland, rich in ragged-robin and buttercups, and with sufficient depth of meadow for the corncrake to run through it with ease, and out of sight. In 1992 the RSPB set up a haven for corncrakes on the island of Coll in the Hebrides

fighting over particularly nectar-rich flower heads. This scene can still be enjoyed in the *Parc National des Cévennes*, where the dominant butterfly, the black-veined white, can be seen by the million in certain years[6] among the crops of ancient cultivated fields. This butterfly has been extinct in England since about 1925 and is currently diminishing its range in north-west Europe.

Another common, but more widespread, butterfly in Europe is the small copper which likes an abundance of flowers especially where there are sandy hot-spots in the crop and field margins. This is just the place, too, to find the common blue with its magnificent iridescent blue uppersides which glint in the sun, a product of refracted light. The meadow brown – appropriately named for meadows – and the wall butterfly are also at home in a flowery cornfield, particularly around the margins. The wall butterfly is a percher which rests with wings outstretched on the hot bare ground and absorbs the sun's energy. Once disturbed, or after having flown off on a sortie against another butterfly which has invaded its airspace, it will return to its original place, or to another strategic place to resume sunbathing. This kind of territorial behaviour is also entertained by several species of skipper butterflies including the small, Essex and grizzled, and they too can become a trifle pugnacious and truculent against intruders. So life carries on in a very exciting manner within and around the cornfield, which by its very structure makes up the seasonal territory which the butterflies defend.

Table 1.3   Butterflies of cornfield margins

Blue, common	*Polyommatus icarus*
Copper, small	*Lycaena phlaeus*
Skipper, Essex	*Thymelicus lineola*
Wall	*Lasiommata megera*
White, black-veined	*Aporia crataegi*
White, marbled	*Melanargia galathea*

The flowers of the cornfield which mean so much to the butterflies are many and various. There are common species and rarer ones, but the commonest are those that have 'corn' in their names. The dominant colours in the paintings of the Impressionists were the reds and yellows which represented the swathes of the corn poppy and the corn marigold. Interspersed with these were the pastel blues of the cornflower ('corn bottle') and the subtle pinky hues of the corncockle, which is sometimes fairly difficult to find in Europe.

The corn poppy is the doyen of all the corn flowers, but not the aristocrat. Its exuberance is far-reaching, its potential to remain dormant in the soil for long periods is great, and its ability to stage a glorious comeback after a long time of dormancy – poppy seed can live up to forty years in its dormant state in the soil – is remarkable.

Cornfield meadows sometimes rich in marbled whites, like this one, *Melanargia galathea*. There are several marbled white species in Europe. Their caterpillars feed on fairly common grasses and the butterfly remains common and widespread

A perceptive description of the flower of the corn poppy was captured by Barclay Wills in his *Downland Treasure*, first published in 1927:

> The big, fat buds of the poppies are very fascinating. A two-piece cap parts suddenly and drops before us. It is stiff and papery; at our touch it crackles or gives a rustling sound as does a one-day growth on a man's chin. The big bud remains, like a blob of red sealing-wax, but presently the petals unfold and droop, and for a time the young flower hangs on its stem like a little skirt of crinkled silk. Gradually the little petals develop and expand, the flower opens and lifts its face toward the sky. A bunch of these beautiful buds is easily carried home inside a bundle of grass; it is quite worth while to bring them![7]

While the corn poppy is perhaps the most obvious flower of the cornfield and elsewhere, the corn marigold can also make a striking spread

There are four species of poppy found as cornfield weeds in Britain, and this is the common one, *Papaver rhoeas*. It may be a southern Mediterranean species, possibly not native to Britain. Seeds are definitely viable in the soil for up to eighty years, maybe over a century

of colour, sometimes without the accompaniment of the corn poppy. It is a sprawling plant which supports plenty of stout little flower heads, and, like the corn poppy, and indeed mallow, is superbly drought-tolerant. These three species, which do not necessarily survive exclusively in cornfields, but can be found in the margins of fields and waste places as well, need a wet spring for establishment of seedlings but thereafter are quite adept at maintaining growth through the early summer to create a dazzling display.

Gardeners who are whipped up with enthusiasm to try and re-create such a gay display of flowers should remember this point when considering water conservation, and remember too that these wild flowers much prefer nutrient-poor soils. The soil of an average garden is nutrient-rich, and not to the liking of most wild flowers of the countryside.

Perhaps the aristocrat of corn flowers is the corncockle, for it is fast becoming an infrequent species. Always aware of the nature of colourful

The corncockle, *Agrostemma githago*, is a relic of the cornfields of western Europe. Its demise, like that of the other corn flowers, is the result of loss of habitat and cleaning of seed

plants in the countryside, A.R. Horwood[8] said earlier this century that 'a district without corn cockle [was] as bad as one in which red campion is absent . . . both are well known favourites.' This is not the case today. Only red campion has survived the passage of time.

Corncockle is a favourite in the wild flower seed business and easy to grow at home in the garden, but the species or variety offered is very different from the real thing in the wild. The treble-sized cultivar sold is called 'Midas'. The wild species is diminutive in size in comparison, up to 0.46 metres tall, its flowers a delicate hue of pink with fairly spiky sepals. To find it in corn is nowadays little short of a miracle of discovery, but, based on my own experience in southern France, it grows in patches and is never taller than the crop. The garden midas is a veritable giant, and when grown at places like Wisley assumes enormous proportions compared to those in the wild. Being a drought-tolerant plant, and having a nutrient-poor soil preference, the plant perhaps excels when pampered, though not all drought-tolerant species do.

This is the 'Midas' cultivar of corncockle grown in gardens, but it differs from the wild form in being a real giant, up to a metre tall, and with more stridently coloured flowers

However beautiful the corncockle, it caused plenty of trouble in Europe in medieval times. The seeds have poisonous chemicals and when milled with corn seeds to make flour present a toxic threat to man once bread has been made. Gastro-enteritis was the disagreeable complaint that everyone in the villages complained about (though not couched in such modern language), and they surely made their grievances and their suggestions known to the village baker, who would have purchased his flour from the mill. The mill-workers would then set about cleaning the corncockle seeds from between the heavy millstones, a laborious process.

The other contender for being the aristocrat of corn flowers is the Venus's-looking-glass, a delightful sprawling plant sometimes found in the presence of candytuft and together the two species look marvellous. I have yet to see it growing in England, though it is present, and it is rarely offered for sale as part of wildflower mixtures. Quite how it got its name is mystifying, but another closely related species occurs in North America.

In France the Venus's-looking-glass is a gem worth seeking, so too the

The meadows of southern France are sometimes pink with wild gladiolus, *Gladiolus illyricus*, here growing with great burnet. In Britain it is a protected and scheduled species and occurs on the Isle of Wight. It is a Red Data Book species too

pheasant's eye, which – only a few centimetres tall, its tiny red eyes being aptly described as pheasant's eyes – enjoys hot patches of bare earth around the margins of fields. In the garden there are named cultivars such as giant pheasant's-eye which rise to a metre under good conditions and must be at least 1 metre taller than the wild species just described.

A dominant meadow plant on the limestone *causses* of southern France are the metre-tall flowering spikes of asphodels, so often unfortunately gathered in armfuls by day-trippers. This perennial lily is a delight in the spring when some quarters are full of these pleasing towering white flowers. At a much lower level, but equally attractive are the swathes of yellow and white iris which adorn the well-grazed and stony ground. Barely 0.3 metres high, these plants (also lilies) seek an existence where many other plants would have difficulty. The biblical lands at the other end of the Mediterranean clearly had their own range of lilies:

Consider the lilies of the field, how they grow; they toil not, neither
   do they spin.
And yet I say unto you, That even Solomon in all his glory was not
   arrayed like one of these.[9]

Today, the margins of cornfields are where wild flowers survive, or where they are reinstated. Efforts by the Game Conservancy over the last decade or so to have the margins of fields made fit for nesting game such as partridge and pheasant have resulted in a wider understanding of the benefits of growing a wider strip of vegetation around a field and giving up a linear unit of crop. The advantages of having beneficial insects and increased productivity in game as an alternative to pest insects and the chemical means to kill them have been widely appreciated. In Germany in certain areas there are now regulations governing the planting of field margins with wild flowers. Gradually the original gene pool represented by the diversity of wild flowers and insects is being conserved, and a natural order of variety will evolve.

Perhaps we have learnt a lesson now that so many of the corn flowers, many now relics of a former age, are found more commonly in gardens than in the countryside, albeit as super-improved varieties and alternative species. The candytuft is an excellent example: it is a vigorous plant of chalky soils, yet it profits well with even more vigour in its 'Little Gem' form, an effervescent plant which overspills rockeries and steps in mounds of white blossom. And how many of us planted cornflowers in the garden when young? They are easy to grow, but how frequently are they now seen in their own niche of a cornfield or waste area?

Notes

1. In Europe 'corn', as in 'cornfields', means various varieties and species of wheat, *Triticum* species, whose seeds are ground for making bread flour. The wild flowers of cornfields refer entirely to those found among this sort of corn. In the United States, and to a lesser extent, Europe too, corn is synonymous with maize, which is *Zea mays*. This is a tall crop which does not have the typical wild flowers associated with cornfields.
2. Roudil, J.L. and Canet, H., 1982.
3. Brandon, P., 1974.
4. Jefferies, Richard, 1925, p. 16.
5. Jefferies, Richard, 1925, pp. 221–6 on 'crakes'. An appreciation of Richard Jefferies's last years in 1885–6 appeared in *Sussex Life* in July 1985, pp. 36–7 under an article entitled 'The naturalist who found hope in the Sussex hills' written by Nicholas Thornton. Jefferies died in his mid-thirties in August 1887.
6. Feltwell, John, 1983.
7. Wills, Barclay, *Downland Treasure*, Methuen, 1927; republished in Beningfield, 1989.
8. Horwood, A.R., 1919.
9. *Matthew*, Chapter 6, verses 28–9.

CHAPTER 2

WATER MEADOWS

Or in my boat I lie
Moored to the cool bank in the summer-heats,
'Mid wide grass meadows which the sunshine fills,
And watch the warm, green-muffled Cumner hills . . .

Matthew Arnold, 'The Scholar Gipsy'

Water meadows are a special type of meadow: they are meadows of quality which are abundant and full and make the sheep get fat. Fabulously rich in plants, they are one of the most endearing and important of all wildlife habitats, conservators' great friends. Wherever the words 'levels', 'brooks', 'lags' or 'washes' are used, water meadows are bound to have been present: they are inextricably part of the colloquial English language.

Technically, there is a difference between water meadows and flood meadows. Flood meadows are low-lying sites which flooded naturally; water meadows are sites whose flooding was engineered by man. Water meadows were also natural alluvial meadows since the flood water brought with it silt, or alluvium.

No wonder Matthew Arnold leant back in his boat and admired the 'green-muffled' Cumner hills in Oxfordshire. He might have done so at Henley-on-Thames or a host of other places along the Thames, or along many of Britain's rivers and streams. It was also the magical water meadow which prompted William Shakespeare to write:

Kissing with golden face the meadows green,
Gilding pale streams with heavenly alchemy;

Sonnet XXXIII

The cuckooflower or lady's-smock, *Cardamine pratensis*, is the mainstay of many a wet and boggy meadow in Europe. Other local names in England and Scotland include meadow flower in Cumbria, meadow pink in Devon and meadow kerses in Dumfries and Galloway

Stratford on the river Avon has always enjoyed its great water meadows. But no longer; the latest survey in Warwickshire shows that, 'the meadows that Shakespeare knew have been reduced to a tiny handful of isolated fragments – only about a dozen top quality meadows remain.'[1]

The gems of meadows left in Britain – the 3 per cent now remaining – are now often conserved by members of the local Wildlife Trusts, of which there are forty-seven affiliated to the Royal Society for Nature Conservation. The following table lists several of their flood meadows which are generally open to the public via the respective trusts:

Table 2.1 Functional Lammas meadows (courtesy Dr A. Brian)

Name of common	County	Hectares
Lugg Meadow (Upper and Lower)[1]	Herefordshire	132
Twyning Great Hay Meadow[2]	Gloucestershire	109
Port Holme[3]	Huntingdonshire	92
Pixey, Yarnton and Oxey Meads[4]	Oxfordshire	c. 85
Powick Hams[5]	Worcestershire	c. 62
Eastwick and Hunsdon Meads[6]	Herts./Middlesex	58
Ogber Mead	Dorset (formerly Hants.)	52
North Meadow, Cricklade[7]	Wiltshire	44
Wick and North Moors, Stogursey[8]	Somerset	37
Upper Ham, Kempsey	Worcestershire	30
Lower Ham, Kempsey	Worcestershire	28
Uckinghall Ham[9]	Worcestershire	28
Hampton Bishop Meadow	Herefordshire	25
Moor Meadow, Bridstow[10]	Herefordshire	18

Additional meadows

Asham Meadow, Birlingham[11]	Worcestershire	26
Gooseham Meadow, Defford[12]	Worcestershire	7

Notes

1. Hereford city bypass is planned to run all along the edge of Upper Meadow very close to the boundary and in places actually in the meadow.
2. Part crossed by M5.
3. Has no commoners, grazing auctioned yearly to one grazier.
4. Part of Pixey Mead is crossed by the Oxford bypass, three-quarters of Oxey Mead is now gravel works.

5. Powick Hams are in several separate bits and each bit is laid up for hay in only certain years in a cycle of three. A four-lane trunk road has recently been built across the meadows on an embankment.
6. Hunsdon Mead is now threatened by a plan for a motorway link road across its centre.
7. Ownership strips on the meadow were reorganized into blocks when the rest of the parish was enclosed.
8. Bounded to the north and *very* close to Hinckley Point nuclear power station.
9. Recently bought by a gravel company which has existing works nearby.
10. Whole meadow ploughed fairly recently. Bounded by recently enlarged A40.
11. Improved grassland, only grazed by owners.
12. Improved grassland, only one owner now, who is also the grazier.

Flood meadows have their own charm. They are lush and lank with heavyweight plants, ripe with water, and colourful too. The fact that they are usually sited within a few metres of a stream or river that annually overflows its banks and spills over the meadow, gives this type of meadow its name. Well-furnished with nutrient-rich silt from the overflowing stream or river, and with their roots kept permanently moist in the soil, the plants do well. This is in great contrast to the cornfields of the previous chapter, which have nutrient-poor soils.

Spring visitors to the Massif Central in France in the Dordogne, Auvergne and the Cévennes will have noticed the meadows besides the streams being white with tiny meadow crocuses mixed with snowdrops – quite a delectable sight. These are rich water meadows, perhaps grazed a little during the summer, but cut for hay during August. The spring flowers are soon overtaken by the floral delights of summer.

In Britain there is only one native meadow crocus, an autumn flowering one, as its name indicates: the meadow saffron, *Colchicum autumnale*. It flourishes well in its remaining woodland and grassland habitats in Herefordshire. But there *is* another meadow crocus in Britain, the autumnal crocus, *Crocus nudiflorus*; this, it is thought, was introduced by the Knights of the Order of St John of Jerusalem, hospitallers from the Mediterranean area. This order of knights were in the habit of dispensing crocus bulbs to their tenants in England. Recent research in Yorkshire and Lancashire has shown that these alien crocuses appear where the original holdings of the knights were located.[2]

If these autumnal crocuses can be associated with the travels of the knights, then it must be said that there is also a suspicion that the

Water meadows were artificially flooded by man using a series of special channels, called carriers, as here in February 1935 near Salisbury, Wiltshire

distribution of another meadow beauty, the pasqueflower, *Anemone pulsatilla*, is related to the distribution of Danish blood. It was probably in the region of Cambridgeshire and Suffolk that this plant acquired its Danish connection as Dane's flower, since it used to be found on the Devil's Dyke and on Fleam Dyke, the earthworks of which are thought to have been associated with the Danes.[3]

The people who worked the land in the past were much more skilled at water and meadow management than we are today. They appreciated the lie of the land, the twisting stream and the rising ground, and schemed many times how the water in a water meadow could be backed up simply by sluicing at a strategic point. In West Sussex the water meadows were contained by the natural lie of the land and were called lags. Long thin ox-bow water meadows followed the course of alder trees lining the streams, and many of their sinuous courses can be seen today simply by regarding the lie of the land. Not all water meadows do this however.

In this tranquil scene, bullocks come down to drink in the shallow stream. Sheep also help to keep rural pastures such as these well grazed, but during winter months the stream is likely to overflow its banks in these low-lying areas and flood the meadows

The water meadows in Hampshire, for instance, used the chalky water of the river Avon, which was flooded over the fields. Channels were cut in fields and up to 20 hectares could be flooded in this way. One great advantage of chalk streams here is that the temperature remains fairly constant at 13°C all year. This relatively warm water encouraged the grass to grow, even in winter, and it did not freeze. Not only was it good for plants, but wintering wildfowl enjoyed sanctuary from other frozen-up areas.

According to some excellent research[4] these working meadows appeared relatively rich in plants, one record for 1888 showing that a meadow at North Charford on the Avon in Hampshire had 88 species of plant of which 26 were grass species. In a late eighteenth-century account of water meadows in southern England (cited Fream, 1888, p. 461):

The herbage of the watered beds is various in species; as ray grass, the meadow poe, the marsh and other bent grasses, and the meadow fescues; the *loliacea* and the *pratensis*, there putting on very different appearances. On the sides of the trenches, and ditches, the flote fescue, reed canary grass (*Phalaris arundinacea*) and the water poe (*Poa aquatica*) are common; also the meadow rue (*Thalictrum flavum*), and the water dock.

In Hampshire, at least, experiments in water meadow management did not really start until the seventeenth century. Their decline occurred at the beginning of this century when cheap grain imports and artificial fertilizers decreased the viability of folding sheep on water meadows.

Grazing stock was taken off during the winter months, and the streams allowed to flood and deposit their vital silt. In the spring, the sluices were raised, the water drained and the spring grass allowed to grow apace. Animals were put on to the meadows to make maximum growth, or the hay was left for harvesting. Everyone got a fair deal. In many communities the fruits of the best water meadows were shared out among the farmers. Everyone had a chance to reap from the best fields in the community. Thus evolved the system of strip-farming, in which each person had a right to a strip of land in every category of field. Boundary markers in the form of large stones were put into the ground and many of these still remain in ancient meadows just where they were placed hundreds of years ago. The sheep also grew fat. Half a hectare of lush water meadow grass would support four hundred ewes and their lambs for one day. Moving them on, securing them in hurdles was all in a day's work for the meadsmen.

Managing water meadows with a complete system of irrigation channels, sluices and water-wheels was mastered very effectively and several good remains of once extensive examples can be found in France. Monks were particularly adept at water mechanics, whether at Battle Abbey in east Sussex, or in the south of France. They had the time, the labour and the diligence. The slowly turning water-wheel was a revolution, in all senses, in getting water from one level to a much higher one. It was cost-effective and needed little maintenance. The wheel scoops water in its buckets at lower levels, then takes it aloft and deposits it into channels, which can be varied in both height and direction, to flow where it is needed.

Around the town of Ganges and in the Cirques des Navacelles (Hérault) water is taken into a conduit for several hundred metres, until it is needed

The water-wheel was fundamental to the well-being of flood meadows, and used water power to carry water up to a different level, and thus via gullies, ditches and carriers to the meadow further downstream in meadows high above the flowing water. Monastic diligence was responsible for channelling the water conduits through the mountains. Not too far away the Pont du Gard (in the *département* of Gard) is an example of precise engineering which allowed the Romans to bring water over several kilometres from the river Gard to Nîmes – thus bringing water to the centre of the town, an incredible feat. The water was used not only for drinking but for gardening.

Cricklade's North Meadow in Wiltshire is famous as an ancient meadow, for it is regarded as having been managed in the same way for about eight hundred years, one of the few places in Britain where strip-farming can still be seen in operation. Here on the banks of the river Thames – which here is just a wee bit too wide to leap across – is a relatively enormous water meadow (some 44 hectares which is equally famous as Britain's foremost snake's-head fritillary meadow. The springtime fritillaries are not found anywhere else in Britain in such numbers, and 80 per cent of the wild British population occurs in this meadow.[5,6]

The meadow management that has allowed North Meadow to be conserved is typical of the ancient system applying to 'Lammas lands'. Such land was grazed by animals from Lammas Day to Lady Day (1 August to 25 March).

There are a number of Lammas meadows remaining in Britain (Table 2.2) but their numbers are threatened and declining as Dr Anthea Brian of the Herefordshire Nature Trust Ltd has found in her extensive studies (Table 2.3). Lammas meadows are typically registered as common land for half the year from about 1 August until 25 March and commoners may exercise their right to graze animals over the whole meadow during this period. Lammas meadows can also be defined as those which are in private ownership between March and August, when the owners grow a hay crop.

Fritillaries are a meadow spectacle in Wiltshire, but not far away in Herefordshire autumnal crocuses thrive in Eades Meadow, though hot summers do not treat the bulbs kindly. Herefordshire has the largest Lammas meadow in Britain – and it is currently under threat of development.

Recent research has shed new light on the possible longevity of meadows and pastures, since grassland has been the predominant type of vegetation on the floodplains of the upper Thames since the clearance of the former alder woodland cover, which probably began in *c.* 3,000 BC. The flood meadows in this area are particularly known for the foxtail

Table 2.2 Meadows managed as Lammas meadows (courtesy Dr A. Brian)

Name of meadow	County	Hectares
Derwent Ings[1]	Yorkshire	*c.* 1,000
Nether Meadow, Loughborough[2]	Leicestershire	120
Severn Ham, Tewkesbury	Gloucestershire	71
Upton Ham, Upton on Severn	Worcestershire	57
Gavern y ddavid, Shocklach Oviat[3]	Cheshire	24
Broad Dales, Gamelsby[4]	Cumbria	*c.* 15
Lammas or Town Meadow, Shelfanger	Norfolk	11
Drigg Holme, Drigg[5]	Cumbria	9
Clifton Ings	Yorkshire	*c.* 24

Notes

1. A very large SSSI area, mainly meadow but some wood and pasture.
2. Parts now enclosed and permanent pasture.
3. There has been recent reorganization and amalgamation of strips and both ends of the meadow are now fenced off and permanent pasture: part of the rest is cut several times a year as silage rather than hay. Flora has lost interest.
4. Parts enclosed and no longer cut for hay.
5. Parts are partly hedged.

Table 2.3 Former Lammas meadows that have ceased to be managed as such recently

Name of meadow	County	Hectares
Barlins and Milhams Meads[1]	Dorset	16
Kings Meads[2]	Hertfordshire	84
Royden and Parndon Meads[3]	Hertfordshire	

Notes

1. Both are crossed by the Christchurch bypass and as a result of its building have ceased to be hay meadows and become pasture or rough grazing.
2. Crossed by A10, four-lane trunk road on flyover, now all rough grazing with about one-eighth hectare of hay.
3. Now permanent pasture.

Silhouetted against the typically flat landscape of a flood meadow, this gnarled and pollarded willow grows at the edge of a ditch at Cricklade

grasses and the great burnet growing together, and in some of these grasslands snake's-head fritillary makes its appearance, as at Cricklade. There is a great possibility that crested dog's-tail and common knapweed meadows have been in existence for the last two thousand years. Thus it is possible that a number of meadows which have been shown by documentary evidence to be up to a thousand years old, may actually be up to two thousand years old, according to the botanical evidence.[7]

The fact that Cricklade survives today is because man has taken off the crop each year, reducing any risk of the meadow being colonized by shrubs and trees. The stone boundary markers are present, and the villagers of Cricklade have been cutting hay regularly on these alluvial soils in the same manner for eight centuries. The only concession today is that a tractor may make the cutting and gathering of hay simpler, where before a farmer with a scythe would work under the blistering summer heat cutting just a few acres a day.

The large flat expanse of meadow at Cricklade looks distinctly un-important at first glance; perhaps, one might think it a large deserted World War II airfield with a nice carpet of dandelions. Timing has to be just right to see the delicate suffusion of pink-purple, almost a purple haze, stretching across the meadow of the fritillaries in full nodding flower. The purple-coloured heads predominate, but there are also attractive white ones, and others of intermediate colour. Then within two weeks, the meadow changes to bright yellow, this time because of dandelion, which seizes the opportunity to break through the flora diversity.

Looking across Cricklade meadow in the spring, one is aware of strips of bright orange where the marsh-marigolds (kingcups) outline extra-damp pockets of water, or splashes of bright yellow where the dyer's greenweed grows in effervescent clumps a metre across and a metre high. Ragged-robin grows where it is less damp. Tall and sprightly, the great burnet stands up in its maroon-mahogany colours in fine fruiting fettle, while furtively hugging the low ground are groves of adder's-tongue fern, an indicator of old meadows.

There can hardly be any better place to reap the joys of the ancient flora of Britain than in the meadows of Cricklade. North Meadow is not far

One of the entrances to North Meadow, Cricklade, famous for its snake's-head fritillaries

from the M4 motorway and worth a visit at any time, attracting over 2,500 visitors a year, mostly during fritillary flowering time. The diversity of wild flowers at Cricklade is exceptional and is exploited commercially. Several wildflower seed merchants sell Cricklade seed mixes.

Some water meadows in England are part of the glebe lands belonging to the church. Since most English villages have evolved around a water source, such as a spring, stream or river, and the church was the centre of the community, it became the norm for the richest landowner, often the church, to own many of the community's water meadows. These there-fore became glebe lands, and it may have been the monks who in fact put in the sluices and organized the proper management of the water levels. Many meadows which are glebe lands have survived through the ages to become important meadows today, unspoilt because of their close bond with the church, and saved from the fate of many low-lying meadows drained to extinction and ploughed for agricultural improvement in the 1960s and 1970s.

Until now, the church has held on to its glebe lands tenaciously, and this has been the meadows' salvation. But now the church is selling off its land, realizing that its previous 'no-sell' policy has reaped dividends in that its holdings now have great conservation appeal. As with hundreds of churchyards in Britain, which were enclosed from the parish's unimproved meadows, church-owned meadows have remained as if in a time-warp, containing flora and fauna which pre-dates those which are found outside their boundaries. Thus it is no surprise to find that the Church Commis-sioners sold off an important site, Glebe Meadows in Warwickshire, to the Warwickshire Nature Conservation Trust – at a price of £20,000 for a 3-hectare meadow.[8]

Threats to water meadows are usually traumatic and irreversible. Habitat destruction at its worst sees their total elimination by grubbing–up and development for industry, urban sprawl, or for shopping centres and malls. There is also outright drainage of water meadows directly, or indirectly, where water authorities pump water from the same ground water supply but from an adjacent site. This indirect form means that drainage is often surreptitious, but it is damaging to the long term status of the water meadow.

Until recent years water authorities in Britain had *carte blanche* to drain the land as they saw fit. The result has been the loss of important wetland

One of the dykes at Amberley Wild Brooks in West Sussex, where the water is controlled by sluices. This wetland habitat was saved from destruction by the people of Amberley, with the help of the Council for the Protection of Rural England, in the 1970s

Drainage ditches like this one in Romney Marsh in Kent used to have water to the rim, so that animals could drink with ease. Now, with decreasing water tables, the water is much further down the edge of the ditch and animals may fall in and drown when they come to drink. This ditch is full of water-crowfoot, *Ranunculus aquatilis*, indicating that it is strongly polluted

areas in places such as Halvergate Marshes (Suffolk) and the Somerset Levels – as well as the vast Caithness peninsula which contains some rich water meadows.

In an effort to bring back some of the thousands of wintering wildfowl which once frequented the Pulborough Brooks in West Sussex, the Royal Society for the Protection of Birds (RSPB) launched an appeal in early 1991 to raise money to manage part of the wetland they bought in this part of the Arun valley. Up to 4,500 wigeon and 2,000 teal used to enjoy the rich grassy meadows, but drainage and river improvements over the last twenty-three years have dried the meadows out and made them unattractive to birds.

In another appeal, started over ten years ago, the RSPB raised £300,000 for the Silver Meadows Appeal, and the money was spent principally on 109 hectares of West Sedgemoor reserves (Somerset) and 37 hectares of the Ouse Washes (Cambridgeshire).[9]

Drainage destroys wetland habitats and their attendant flora and fauna for ever

All good farmers drain land; in the recent past in England they were paid to do so, and it does make good farming sense to drain wet land. Unfortunately, because of this water meadows have always been vulnerable to damage, and even their accompanying habitats, the wet woodlands – important habitats in their own right – have suffered from felling, grubbing-out, drainage, and general 'improvement'.

Ploughing and the application of herbicides and fertilizers are both damaging procedures which will kill the meadow diversity overnight. It is sad when beautiful meadows change from a pretty sight to a totally uninteresting monoculture of rye grass in one season.

When ragged-robin, *Lychnis flos-cuculi*, has the perfect habitat, it will become rampant. Sadly, in today's world its habitats are severely disrupted and only single stems of this charming species can be found. White forms are also known

Wetland habitats, be they water meadows, wet woodland, bogs, fens or marshes, are all vulnerable to drainage and the drying-up of the land. Plant species which are entirely dependent upon water for their existence, become localized in isolated outposts of wet habitats. Conservationists treat them as precious vestiges of typical, indicative, species of wetland.

Fens are particularly important habitats in their own right. They are places where peat overlays chalk or calcareous rock, and they have interesting ecological associations. The relatively few fens which remain in

Britain harbour a diminishing number of important species. The local or declining 'fen meadow species' in Britain include the bog pimpernel, bogbean, marsh valerian, water avens, southern marsh–orchid and ragged–robin.

Many fens, and their flora and fauna, exist on a delicate knife–edge, courtesy of the controlled water table. In the case of the large water dock, a large dock species which grows directly out of shallow water, it is maintained simply by regulating the water level. The plant is the caterpillar food of the large copper butterfly, *Lycaena dispar*, a butterfly which graced some wetlands, water meadows and fens up to 1851 when the last British specimen was recorded. After the English sub-species became extinct efforts were made to establish a Dutch sub-species of the butterfly in the fenland. The butterfly succeeded for a number of years, first in 1927 at Woodwalton Fen, then in 1942 at Wicken Sedge Fen. It again died out but was established again, only to be extinguished by a flood in 1968. Correct management of the watery habitat was always essential, and it was found necessary to bring indoors for the winter all the small larvae, which normally hatch in late summer, to increase their chances of survival through to the following year.

Another interesting butterfly which frequents the fenland water meadows is the common swallowtail, *Papilio machaon*. It is a large yellow and black butterfly which lays its eggs upon another water-dependent plant, milk parsley – so named because it exudes a whitish fluid from joints in its stems. The butterfly is protected by the Wildlife and Countryside Act 1981, and is conserved on Wicken Sedge Fen. The English species is a little different from its continental relatives, since it has more orange markings and does not lay its eggs on fennel or wild carrot as others are inclined to do.

Wicken Sedge Fen may be a gem in the world of Britain's wetland habitats in the south, but the prize for the smallest nature reserve in Britain, and the habitat of one of Britain's rarest plants, goes to a nature reserve only the size of a room near Cheltenham in Gloucestershire. The speciality in this tiny meadow is a moisture-loving buttercup called the Badgeworth buttercup, *Ranunculus ophioglossifolius*, otherwise known more correctly as the adder's-tongue spearwort.

A particularly attractive violet of the fenland, and also of the limestone pavement of County Clare, Eire – two apparently dissimilar habitats – is the fen violet. It has always been a speciality of the fenland, like the raft

Meadowsweet, *Filpendula ulmaria*, only grows where it is damp, and is common in wet meadows and along roadsides near ditches. It used to be called 'queen of the meadow' and 'lady of the meadow' in North America

A crofter in the Aran Islands, County Clare, Eire, making baskets from willows, which grow alongside ditches in wet meadows

spider, but in Eire its preferred micro-habitat is under the branches of shrubby cinquefoil.

In the United States three groups of wetland plants which are particularly under threat because of habitat destruction, drainage and collectors, are the Venus's fly trap, *Drosera* sp. (there are five American species), and the pitcher plant, of which there are species belonging to the *Sarracenia* and *Darlingtonia* genera. William Robinson, the celebrated gardener, writer, botanist and traveller visited the Sierras of California in the late nineteenth century especially to see pitcher plants, as he described:

One of my objects of coming here was to see the California pitcher-plant (Darlingtonia) in a wild state. This plant resembles the

Sarracenias of the east side of the continent. . . . I came upon the Darlingtonias, greatly to my satisfaction, on the north side of a hill, at an elevation of about 4,000 feet, growing among Ledum bushes, and here and there in sphagnum, and presenting at a little distance the appearance of a great number of Jargonelle pears.[10]

Today conservationists look after the Venus's fly traps and the pitcher plants, often in the relative protection of nature reserves. It is now more likely that reserve wardens or members of the Sierra Club or Audubon Society will escort visitors to see these gems, since these plants are not so common as they were when Robinson saw them.

Of the remaining water and flood meadows in England and Wales there are many which have been conserved, either as part of National Nature Reserves, trust reserves, or as (or as well as being) Sites of Special Scientific Interest (SSSIs). North Meadow, Cricklade, is deemed sufficiently important to be granted status as a National Nature Reserve (NNR).[11]

Meadow loss in Britain

The data used here is drawn principally from the Royal Society for Nature Conservation's 1991 publication *Vanishing Meadows*. It is current up to the end of 1990 and emcompasses all different types of meadows. It is reproduced here for two reasons: first, the data rarely reaches a wide audience, and second, the results of this meadow survey are so shocking that everyone should take positive action now to do something to halt the tragic decline of meadows. Our meadow heritage is literally likely to disappear down the drain. Expressing the data in this way helps to reinforce the problem and to emphasize meadow loss at a local level. Everyone should take note. (Numbers on map correspond to numbers in notes below.)

1. **Avon** The remaining meadows have so far escaped developers although agricultural operations remain a threat.
2. **Bedfordshire** Only 76 areas of meadowland remain, most being steeply sloping chalk downland. Off the chalk escarpments meadows cover only 155 hectares.
3. **Berkshire** Only 0.33 per cent of the chalk outcrop remains as meadowland.
4. **Birmingham and the Black Country** Meadows do remain, but few are particularly rich in wildlife.
5. **Buckinghamshire** The Vale of Aylesbury was one of the richest areas for meadows in the country – now all but a handful have been lost.
6. **Cambridgeshire** Only 386 hectares of meadow of wildlife value on chalk downland remain.
7. **Cheshire** Only about 150 meadows remain, occurring as tiny isolated pockets surrounded by intensively farmed land.

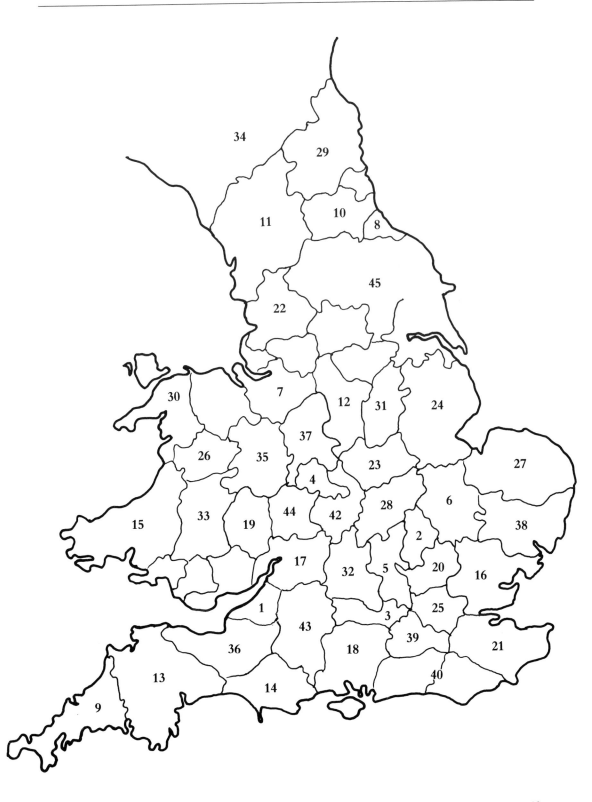

8. **Cleveland**   Only 36 areas of meadow now have significant wildlife value.
9. **Cornwall**   Meadows are exceptionally rare.
10. **County Durham**   In Weardale a 1986/7 NCC survey of hay meadows showed that out of 328 fields only 45 were of significant wildlife value.
11. **Cumbria**   A few isolated examples of meadows still exist in the west of the county and in the south-east inside the Yorkshire Dales National Park.
12. **Derbyshire**   In the Erewash Valley the rate of meadow loss is accelerating: green-winged orchids are extinct in the county.
13. **Devon**   65 per cent of the 'rhos' pastures of the Culm outside SSSIs was destroyed between 1984 and 1989 with losses exceeding 90 per cent in some localities.
14. **Dorset**   Only 350 hectares of meadowland remain on neutral soils – 60 per cent less than in 1983.
15. **Dyfed**   In an area noted for the predominance of meadows the rate of destruction is rapid.
16. **Essex**   A meadow survey in 1985 showed that only 90 meadows of significant wildlife value remained in the county and these are all small and isolated fragments.
17. **Gloucestershire**   A single meadow remains in the Forest of Dean, a handful survive in the Severn Vale, and in the Cotswolds they are declining at an alarming rate due to neglect.
18. **Hampshire and the Isle of Wight**   Watership Down, made famous by Richard Adams in his book of that name, was a single block of chalk downland covering 528 hectares in 1873: only 16 hectares of species-rich turf remains today – in 15 small fragments. Snake's-head fritillaries are now confined to a single meadow.
19. **Herefordshire**   The largest surviving Lammas meadow in the country is under threat.
20. **Hertfordshire**   Only 43 hectares of chalk meadowland of wildlife value remain.
21. **Kent**   Away from chalk downland only about 70 meadows now exist in Kent.
22. **Lancashire**   Less than 200 hectares of meadow remain on neutral soils.
23. **Leicestershire**   On oolitic limestone only 28 hectares of meadowland remain, fragmented into 12 sites. Green-winged orchids are confined to 12 meadows on neutral soils.
24. **Lincolnshire**   The remaining high quality meadows can be counted on the fingers of two hands: most are protected as Trust nature reserves.
25. **London**   Meadows are being destroyed by development, golf courses and lack of management.
26. **Montgomeryshire**   Only 39 remaining meadows are known to be of high wildlife value, 21 of which are designated SSSIs.
27. **Norfolk**   Only 8 per cent of meadows retain any significant wildlife interest, most being in river valleys and on spring lines.
28. **Northamptonshire**   Only 8 hectares of meadows on limestone remain and there are now less than a dozen water meadows in the county.
29. **Northumberland**   In South Tynedale, only 60 of the 697 hectares of hay meadows surveyed by the NCC had significant conservation value.
30. **North Wales**   Surveys in the 1980s showed that 49 per cent of meadows were being invaded by scrub or bracken.
31. **Nottinghamshire**   As long ago as 1977 a survey of 1,500 grass fields found only 5

to be of high conservation value. In the 518 square kilometres of the Trent Valley only 5 hay meadows and 1 water meadow remain.

32. **Oxfordshire**   Few patches of downland larger than 5 hectares remain.

33. **Radnorshire**   Neutral meadows are disappearing at a rate of 11 per cent per annum. The globeflower is threatened with extinction.

34. **Scotland**   By 1984 Scottish primroses grew on only 15 coastal Orkney sites and had disappeared from inland areas as a result of changing agricultural practices. In Ayrshire only 0.001 per cent of the county is meadowland.

35. **Shropshire**   In the Clee Hills area 50 per cent of lowland meadows of significant conservation value was lost between 1979 and 1989. In the Stiperstones area 51 per cent was destroyed between 1979 and 1991.

36. **Somerset**   Within the Exmoor National Park a comprehensive survey found that at least 92 per cent of meadows had been lost since the 1930s and in the Blackdown Hills only 2 per cent of grasslands in the proposed AONB had any ecological interest.

37. **Staffordshire**   Less than 150 meadows remain.

38. **Suffolk**   Meadows with some wildlife value cover only 1.6 per cent of the county.

39. **Surrey**   Only 50 hectares of meadowland on neutral or acid soil remained in 1978: this is likely to have fallen to 40 hectares today. Even chalk downland, for which Surrey is famous, is now reduced to only 288 hectares.

40. **Sussex**   A 1990 survey of 1,000 grassland sites in the Weald of East Sussex showed only 41 meadows containing semi-natural vegetation, of which only 18 were of significant conservation value.

41. **Ulster**   The scale of meadow loss is unknown as surveys are not complete. In the Glens of Antrim AONB only one top quality meadow remains.

42. **Warwickshire**   The meadows that Shakespeare knew have been reduced to a tiny handful of isolated fragments – only about a dozen top quality meadows remain.

43. **Wiltshire**   Only 71 hay and water meadows of high wildlife value were found in a 1984–5 survey. 80 per cent of the wild British population of snake's-head fritillary now grows in one meadow in Wiltshire.

44. **Worcestershire**   33 per cent of meadows present in 1978 have now been destroyed, yet Worcestershire is probably the richest lowland county in the country for meadows.

45. **Yorkshire**   Northern chalk meadowland covered extensive areas of Lincolnshire and East Yorkshire but is now limited to a few areas in the Yorkshire Wolds, where only 200 hectares remain outside SSSIs.

One English county, Hampshire, which has researched its meadow heritage has found that there are seven types of meadow present, many of them wet and watery: coastal meadows, river-flood plain meadows, marshy meadows, peaty meadows, dry loamy meadows, wet loamy/sandy meadows and clay meadows.[12] Evidence in the Domesday Book shows that there were once extensive areas of Hampshire that were cleared as meadows. Teams of eight oxen used to plough the land needed 8 tons of hay each winter for sustenance. The hay meadows were cut out along the major rivers such as the Avon, Lower Test and the Itchin. Villagers drew lots to manage some of the better fertile meadows, thus the custom in the period of the Domesday of 'Lot' or 'Dole' Meadows. Up to the 1830s water meadows were quite common along these river valleys, but many were improved and ploughed, thus destroying their semi-natural qualities. In the 1980s only 20 hectares of these unimproved meadows survived, and Hampshire's ancient meadows are now in serious need of conservation.

Notes

1. Royal Society for Nature Conservation, 1991, pp. 10–11.
2. Marshall, A., 1991, pp. 33–4.
3. Grigson, G., 1958, p. 42.
4. Doherty, J., 1985.
5. Gibbons, B., 1990, pp. 216–18.
6. Hopkins, J.J., 1990, pp. 202–13. Hopkins also draws attention to other important meadows in Oxfordshire, Pixey and Yarnton Meads, which have an ancient system of management.
7. Lambrick, G. and Robinson, M., 1988, pp. 55–75 and Rackham, O., 1988, pp. 3–6.
8. Committee for Environmental Education, *Habitat*, Vol. 27, No. 5, 1990, pp. 4–5.
9. Thanks to Bob Scott of the RSPB for this information.
10. Robinson, W., 1879, p. 150. *Ledum* is a genus of North American shrub which lives in sphagnum bogs.
11. Nature Conservancy Council, 1988.
12. Hazel, V., 1984.

CHAPTER 3

COWSLIP MEADOWS

I know a bank whereon the wild thyme blows,
Where oxlips and the nodding violet grows,

William Shakespeare, *A Midsummer Night's*
Dream, II. i. 249.

Cowslips have always been associated with old meadows. This is because
cowslip meadows were once plentiful and the flowers were abundant and
could easily be gathered by the armful. To William Shakespeare the
English countryside in the spring would have been full of cowslips.
Everyone seems to have picked cowslips in the past, including children and
gypsies who sold them in the street.[1]

Cowslip posies might be very endearing, but collecting is really frowned
upon today. The only real exception, if there is one at all, is for children,
inveterate pickers, but they should pick only those plants that they have
personally planted – and the 'pick and plant' motto should be exercised
only in school grounds or in their gardens at home; otherwise, the habit of
picking would be continued in the wild, and the difference between
sensitive species and common species would not be respected or understood.

The *Primula* genus to which cowslips belong has representatives which
live in all continents, but the cowslip is particularly typical to Europe and in
Asia. Members of this genus are only natives in the northern hemisphere,
but have been introduced to many other countries, especially as cultivars in
gardens. The kind of meadow that cowslips grow in best is one which is
described as basic, particularly those containing calcareous soils. In
England the cowslip enjoys the chalky downs typical of southern England,
but it is equally at home in the wet streamside meadows of France, where it
is not particularly basic. Both meadows and pastures are suitable habitats

Miriam Rothschild's carpet of cowslips in early May

for cowslips, and the traditional management of these habitats, keeping them open, is ideal for the prosperity of cowslips. In Europe the cowslip is generally well distributed; it starts to decline within Arctic meadows, and is absent from some parts of Scotland and Ireland.

In country villages during the last century it was not uncommon to make cowslip balls, as Flora Thompson recalls in her *Lark Rise to Candleford*.

Cowslip balls were made for the children. These were fashioned by taking a great fragrant handful of the flowers, tying the stalks tightly with string, and pulling down the blooms to cover the stems. The bunch was then almost round, and made the loveliest ball imaginable.[2]

As well as making cowslip balls, people made cowslip wine by fermenting the blossoms with sugar. The resulting alcoholic concoction was used as a domestic soporific and as an anodyne.[3] The recipe quoted here from a nineteenth-century recipe is typical:

> To every gallon of water put three pounds of loaf sugar; boil the quantity half an hour, taking off the scum as it rises. When cool, put to it a crust of toasted bread dipped in thick yeast, let the liquor ferment in a tub for thirty-six hours; then put into the cask, for every gallon, the peels of two lemons and the rind of one, together with the peel and rind of a Seville orange, and one gallon of cowslip pips. Pour the liquor on these, stir every day, carefully, for a week; then to every three gallons put a pint of brandy. Stop the cask close, and leave it undisturbed for six weeks, at the end of which time the wine may be bottled off.[4]

The passion for picking cowslips and primroses captivated the Victorians, who neither considered aspects of conservation (which were then in their infancy), nor had any qualms about raiding woods and digging up all interesting plants, especially ferns. With the creation of the railway network in Britain, many people had the first opportunity to go far afield and collect. And the collecting mania existed well into this century. There were 'daffodil specials' laid on by the Great Western Railway, and on one Easter Sunday 1934, a train travelled from Paddington in London to Gloucester. Here the eager passengers disembarked and spent the rest of the day tearing up as many daffodils as they could find.[5] On other excursions primroses and bluebells suffered as well as the snake's-head fritillary and the pasqueflower, both of which are hardly seen outside their rare localities today, only in gardens.

Picking or cutting (or for that matter, mowing) does not have the damaging effect on plant populations as pulling and digging up can do, and bluebells have probably fared much better than members of the primrose family. It is hard to dislodge a bluebell carpet, short of grubbing everything out and burning as the bulbs lie 15–25 cm below the surface.

The cowslip, as referred to in Europe, is known by its Latin name of *Primula veris* and belongs to the primrose family. Its close ally, the primrose, *Primula vulgaris* (*vulgaris* meaning common), often occurs in the same meadow and occasionally hybrid forms occur between the two. Thus a false oxlip is produced (*Primula veris x vulgaris*) which has primrose-like flowers on long cowslip-like stems. There is another true species which is similar, to confuse further, and this is the oxlip, *Primula elatior*, but the false oxlip can be separated from this because it never grows in large clumps, the stems are shorter and the leaves taper towards the base. Cowslips and primroses may be the meadow norm in Britain, but in Bavaria and in the Tyrol the meadow norm is the oxlip.

Cowslip is really a polite way of saying 'cowslop', a fifteenth-century name mentioned in herbals, for the plant was thought to emanate from places where cows splattered the ground with their cowpats.[6] This would seem to indicate that cowslips were indeed associated with pastures, rather than meadows. However, in those early times there was probably no real distinction between these two types of field management, since pastures were probably just as flowery as hay meadows.

A great lover of chalk and limestone, cowslips grow particularly well on the Downs and Chilterns of southern England, where they can be quite miniature (less than 2.5 centimetres tall) and where they spend their lives being trampled underfoot and frequently nibbled. Alternatively, the cowslip can grow ten times taller in lush, unimproved meadows by the side of babbling brooks, and altogether assume a much grander form. Its nodding head of flowers becomes much more apparent, like a bunch of keys, and it was this that gave it its association with St Peter, with his keys to heaven. The cowslip enjoys a distribution throughout western Europe as far south as the Mediterranean, but excluding the northern part of Fennoscandia.

In nineteenth-century books, the cowslip was occasionally referred to as an auricula. Auriculas (*Primula auricula*), related to the cowslip, are rather well-prized in English gardens, but they are native to the mountains of central Europe. I have seen sheets of yellow auriculas in Alpine meadows and on almost inaccessible Alpine scree slopes – where the best always survive, away from man's possessive fingers – and they grow in groups

Oxlips, *Primula elatior*, smother these Alpine pastures in the Austrian Tyrol

poking their way through the April snows and avalanches at 900–1200 metres.

One place where auriculas are protected is the Karwendel Nature Protection Area, a part of the Tyrol in northern Austria. In the valley plains the auriculas grow on grazed pastures and are small in comparison to their leafy fellows on vertical surfaces. The auricula is commonly known as bear's ears, because of the shape of its leaves. It is also called the precipice plant. This rocky environment recalls the limestone of the Burren where another superb primula, the fairy foxglove, *Erinus alpinus*, makes its own pink sheets of meadow over whatever piece of rocky surface it chooses. The fairy foxglove is a speciality of Western Ireland, but in Scotland the primrose has decreased to only fifteen coastal sites on the island of Orkney.

The auricula was eagerly sought and hybrids raised in the sixteenth century since it was a favourite mountain plant that adapted well to the garden. During the Civil War, Sir Thomas Hanmer grew forty named varieties of auricula in his garden in North Wales.[7] Attention was focused on the sort of soil that auriculas liked, or so it was thought:

> consisting of goose dung, steeped in bullock's blood with two parts of baker's sugar scum, two parts of night soil, three parts of yellow loam taken from molehills and a quantity of sea sand.

In the New World the cowslip was a completely different plant, at least to look at; indeed the only connection the American cowslip has with the European one is that it is a member of the same primrose family. The American cowslip, or shooting star, of which there are fourteen species, belongs to the genus *Dodecatheon*. A handful of these are grown in English gardens. Clusters, or flowers, grow on long stems in the spring and eventually turn from being pendulous to being upright, thus earning themselves the name of 'shooting stars'.[8]

That cowslips and primroses are visited by insects, especially bumble-bees, is well-known, certainly to writers, but they are not visited in the large numbers that other springtime flowers like lesser celandine or spring cinquefoil are. True, as Shakespeare wrote:

> Where the bee sucks, there suck I:
> In a cowslip's bell I lie,[9]

or, as Keats enquired,

> Would be to find where violet beds were nestling,
> And where the bee with cowslip bells was wrestling[10]

but honey-bees do not trouble too much with primroses or cowslips and they are not significant nectar sources.[11] This is despite the fact that cowslips have a delightful scent, typical of the smell of spring.

It is curious that both Shakespeare and Keats should associate the honey-bee with the cowslip since they would not appear to have been evolved for each other. The structure of cowslip flowers – the bells – would only be welcoming to an insect with a long tongue, which the honey-bee does not possess. However, the honey-bee is a persistent insect and will probe through the lower part of the bell to seek nectar when it

Black-veined whites, *Aporia crataegi*, fight for possession of these scabious flowers

wants to, a trick which it also does with the bluebell. In the bluebell the petals are held close together and the bee pushes its tongue between the tight-fitting parts of the bell.

Like the primrose, the cowslip has two sorts of flower, some with short stamens and a long style (pin-eyed) and others with long stamens and a short style (thrum-eyed). Each plant has only one sort of flower, a device to ensure that cross-pollination occurs. An important pollinator in the spring, with a tongue long enough to penetrate the flower tube to the nectaries situated at the base, is the brimstone butterfly, *Gonepteryx rhamni*, which has the same colour wings as the primroses. It is fascinating to see the brimstone working the springtime woods before the leaves have broken out on the trees, working its way from one clump of butter-coloured flowers to the next.[12] The co-evolved system between plant and butterfly is so well executed that cross-pollination is ensured whichever way the plants are visited, thrum before pin or vice versa, such is the way that the stamens and style are arranged.

There is one charming little butterfly, with an aristocratic name, which

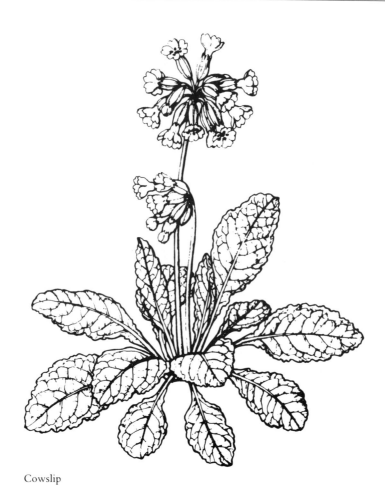

Cowslip

lays its eggs only on cowslip leaves and is thus dependent upon the success of cowslips. Its name is the Duke of Burgundy fritillary, *Hamearis lucina*. Less frequently seen in Britain than before, this little butterfly – it is no more than 34 mm with wings outstretched – is protected on some nature reserves in Britain though it is fairly widespread in the rest of Europe.

Many thousands of cowslip meadows have disappeared in the last few decades in Britain. A typical example was the loss of the 'paigle' meadow in the Alkham Valley near Dover in 1977 when the whole area was bulldozed to destruction. The loss of cowslips and primroses is mostly permanent, though there are chances for reinstatement of habitat if it is not under concrete or water, but the general trend does not look helpful. No wonder Gail Vines in 1983[13] had this to say about English meadows:

HRH Prince Charles, pictured in 1985, in the wild flower meadow created for him in the grounds of his country house, Highgrove in Gloucestershire

The meadows of Britain are turning into gravel pits, ploughed fields or urban sprawl at a tremendous rate. Even 30 years ago, much of lowland Britain was still covered by pastures and meadows filled with buttercups, cuckoo-flowers and cowslips.

The decline in the fortunes of cowslip meadows is the result of 'improvement' of land through ploughing, use of herbicides and straight habitat loss to urban and commercial development. Where cowslips have remained in southern Europe they have often suffered from long term drainage which dries out the meadows. However, there seems to be a natural variation in the abundance of cowslips – some years familiar cowslip meadows seem even more floriferous than before – so a decrease in numbers 'in the wild' should not be regarded as an immediate sign of a decline in their fortune. I write 'in the wild' but it is worth stressing that cowslips and primroses appear courtesy of a habitat cleared by man and his grazing beasts. If it were not for man, primroses would be confined to the mossy banks and waysides in woodland clearings. Alpine meadows and lower level meadows would be the poorer.

The great advantage of most primulas is that they are good germinators, and success can be achieved readily in the re-creation of cowslip meadows and pastures. There are several good examples in Northamptonshire. It has even been known for someone with a love of wild flowers in their heart to sprinkle 10 kilogrammes of cowslip seed from a light aeroplane over the downland that they manage! Not all conservationists would be amused.

One who has taken positive steps over the last decade or so to promote the welfare of the humble English cowslip is Miriam Rothschild. She farms in the alluvial soils of Northamptonshire and currently has 222 hectares under cowslip.[14] The cowslips are grown as one might find them in the wild and also in strips in well-weeded rows. Here their main purpose is to provide seed for the wildflower seed market. Seeds from Dr Rothschild's Sudborough and Ashton fields have been incorporated into seed mixes which have blossomed at Highgrove, the country home of Their Royal Highnesses, The Prince and Princess of Wales in Gloucestershire, along motorway embankments and in countless other places in Britain.

Notes

1. In Britain it is not illegal to pick cowslips, but it is illegal to dig them up. On nature reserves they are protected like all flora and fauna and should not be picked or dug up. It is only legal to dig up *any* plant in Britain if you are the owner or occupier, or have the owner's permission, provided these plants are not listed in the Wildlife and Countryside Act, 1981, or if a tree has a tree preservation order on it..
2. Thompson, F., 1977, p. 117.
3. Ogilvie, J., 1888.
4. Anonymous, 1866.
5. Sheail, J., 1976, p. 6.
6. Grigson, G., 1958, pp. 285–6.
7. Fisher, J., 1985, p. 32.
8. *Hortus Third* lists other 'cowslips', such as *Caltha palustris*, which is a surprise to any European who knows it as marsh–marigold (but it is also called 'Meadow-bright' which is very appropriate), as well as *Mertensia virginica*. Just to completely confuse matters in the USA this latter species is also called 'Virginia cowslip' and 'Bluebell'.
9. Shakespeare, W., *The Tempest*, V. i. 88–9.
10. Barnard, John, ed., *John Keats, The Complete Poems*, 1973, p. 52, John Keats To George Felton Mathew.
11. Howes, F.N., *Plants and Beekeeping*. London, Faber & Faber, 1979, p. 185.
12. It would appear that I have been extremely fortunate in this sighting, since, having spoken with other naturalists, it seems this observation is not at all common.
13. Vines, G., 1983, p. 486.
14. Rothschild, M., 1991, personal communication.

CHAPTER 4

HAY MEADOWS

Upon the grass no longer hangs the dew
Forth lies the mower, with his glittering scythes,
In snowy shirt bedight all unbraced,
He moves athwart the mead with sidling bend,
And lays the grass in many a swathey line:
In every field, in every lawn and meadow,
The rousing voice of industry is heard;
The haycock rises, and the frequent rake
Sweeps on the fragrant hay in heavy wreaths.

Joanna Baillie (1762–1851), 'Hay Making'

Of all the uses of meadows, haymaking is the most widespread and the most important. It is immaterial where the meadow is, whether it is in lowland, upland or by the side of a stream, although its situation and fertility certainly affects the quality of the hay. Water meadows can therefore be fine hay meadows.

The smell of new-mown hay is incredibly evocative, caused principally by the juices which exude from sweet vernal grass when it is cut, most notably by the chemical courmarin. It is this smell which imparts the English countryside in summer.

The aroma of new-mown hay was not the only pleasure people had from their own meadows in the past. They also took hay plants to bed with them to make stuffing material. Thus bedstraw and woodruff, both of which have the same aromatic qualities when dried, were used for bedding material. Bedstraw was also good for keeping fleas and other insects in the bed at bay. There is a tradition that bedstraw was also good to put in the bed for women in labour, thus lady's bedstraw, *Galium verum*.

There is nothing quite like lying down in a herb-rich meadow on a

The foamy flowers of bedstraw flourish in this poor soil in southern France, together with poppies and candytuft

drowsy day in summer – the kind of thing that Jerome K. Jerome might have done, or as Keats wrote:

> O who wouldn't stop in a meadow?
> O [who] would not rumple the daisies there,
> And make the wild fern for a bed do?[1]

There also used to be a custom of 'finishing' racehorses old pastures so that they ate particular wild flowers which gave them extra essential nutrients.

One particular trace element, molybdenum, was not wanted since this gave livestock severe digestive problems and had to be remedied with copper sulphate; that was in the late 1940s. Such pastures were called 'teart' pastures and were found in parts of Somerset, Gloucestershire and Warwickshire, and plants such as purging flax, *Linum catharticum*, and carnation flax, *Carex panicea*, were blamed. It was believed that molybdenum in Yorkshire-fog, a very common grass, was responsible.[2]

A gang of four cut the hay, making light work with their two-handled scythes. Refreshments are at hand for a break when their curved blades need to be honed to razor sharpness

The most romantic idyll of the hay meadow conjured up in the imagination is probably of a small parcel of land surrounded by thick hedgerows dripping with May blossom and entered by a little rickety farm gate. The view from the gate over the meadow would have been rich and full in the spring. Though many meadows were just like this in old England, there would also have been long thin water meadows following the contours of the land, and these meadows would have been quite big, perhaps 2 kilometres long.

Scythes could be used in these small meadows where present-day tractors cannot reach. Those tiny hay meadows, perhaps on difficult slopes in upland areas, were ideal for the swish of the huge blade through the hay. The scyther's job was a skilled one, passed on from father to son. The blade was always honed sharp and attached to this was a long handle which had to be held in two hands, and was fashioned out of ash cut from the hedgerow.

Ash was used for tools since it is extremely tolerant to being bent, but in North America the appropriate wood for these characteristics was found to be hickory. The shape of the handle – or snaith, or snead – varied according to the part of the country, typically being strongly curved in southern

England, less curved in the Lake District, while in Scandinavia it was straight. The curve was incorporated into the wood by first steaming the freshly cut and de-barked piece of wood, and then bending it around suitably-aligned pegs set in a large wooden framework. After the handle had dried sufficiently it could be put into the head of the scythe blade.

Like so many other tasks on the farm, haymaking was labour-intensive and so all the family would turn out for reaping, stooking and stacking the hay. One can almost see the scene, with labourers in old English smocks, leather belts and straw hats, and small children running amok. Cider flowed freely; scything was thirsty work. Members of extended families, brothers and uncles would join forces to help scythe each other's fields, working through a few acres each day. The women, boys and girls would work behind the men, gathering up the hay and stooking it to dry. There would always be a race against time when the weather looked forbidding and menacing on the horizon, a situation quite familiar today.

It was essential to gather the hay in before the weather broke, especially, as here, in England, so often all who could lent a hand. Communal spirit is widespread, and in Finland this kind of voluntary work among neighbours was called '*Talkoo*' work

Just as the scythe's style is attributable to a region or country, so too are the sheaves, stooks and even the haystacks and ricks. Several bundles, or sheaves, of hay would be stood up against each other in the form of a stook of hay. Both hay and corn were cut and stooked, but it was more usual for corn to be treated in this way. The hayrick or haystack often had regional characteristics. They ranged from relatively uninteresting rectangular or square shapes to the small hay domes of County Clare in western Eire. Sadly the haystack is in danger of dying out, since for decades hay has had no value as a bedding for animals which are now increasingly kept during winter on concrete floors. During the 1960s to 1980s excess hay from cornfields was burnt, giving rise to appalling palls of smoke over the countryside, often drifting over towns and cities, but now stubble-burning is being outlawed. The most modern treatment of hay is to bale it into huge square 'bales', which is a change from the large round 'bales' which littered the vast cornfields of England during the 1980s – many of them just stacked at the field's margin to rot, or baggaged into black plastic sacks to make silage.

Haystacks on a farmstead overlooking Galway Bay, County Clare, Eire. The small thatched cottages of County Clare have small meadows enclosed by stone walls

The old words associated with haymaking are interesting. The words 'snaith' and 'snead', as used for a scythe handle, come from the Anglo-Saxon 'sneadan' which means to cut. Though scythes were the usual means of cutting hay, hand-held sickles were also used to cut small amounts. Towards the end of the eighteenth century the word to 'shear' was used for the cutting of grass or corn, though its usage today is more associated with cutting wool from sheep; thus a 'shearer' then was a reaper of standing crops.

Gleaning the fields and vineyards was a time-honoured occupation of the poor people of each village, who usually had the right to wander over land once the crop had been taken, whether it was corn, hay, grapes or soft fruits. There were always discarded spoils which would be useful for someone, if only to feed the chickens or the cottage pig. The ears of corn which had fallen off were particularly valuable and would be eagerly

Gleaning the fields was a common practice, not only used by the poor to find ears of corn, but to fatten pigs, poultry and bullocks. Here, on 14 September 1950, young turkeys (gobblers) take to the fields of stubble at Hallsand in south Devon

gathered up to make flour. Hay would be gathered as a bedding for animals and to put on the earthen floors of the cottages.

Most hay meadows were not ploughed, but occasionally they may have been in order to grow a good stand of corn. Teams of oxen would be led into the meadow to turn the sods of soil and expose the rich soil. By always ploughing a field in one direction the sods of soil were always thrown to one particular side, and this gradually influenced the look of the land. The field started to look undulated and to take on the 'ridge and furrow' form of the traditionally ploughed field that we recognize today. Today there are many tens of thousands of these fields on which ploughing has long been abandoned, but the tell-tale undulations, seen particularly with a dusting of snow which falls into the hollows, or with the shadows from a setting sun, can be very obvious.

The typical length worked by a team of oxen was a furrow-length, in today's parlance a 'furlong'. One furlong was 220 yards, or 10 chains (a chain being 22 yards) and since that length, and multiples of it, was used for measuring and establishing hedgerows, fascinatingly its historic influence can still be seen today in the framework of fields, meadows and hedgerows.

Work on a typical English farmstead centred around the productivity of its surrounding meadows and pastures as Flora Thompson, describing a typical Tudor farmstead, wrote in *Lark Rise to Candleford*:

> The meadows around the farmstead sufficed for the carthorses' grazing and to support the store cattle and a couple of milking cows which supplied the farmer's family and those of a few of his immediate neighbours with butter and milk. A few fields were sown with grass seed for hay, and sainfoin and rye were grown and cut green for cattle food.[3]

The patchwork nature of the English countryside is a result of meadows and pastures being part of the small field system created by the extensive Enclosure Acts.[4] Although a great many of these original meadows and pastures have disappeared during the last few decades, strenuous efforts have been made to conserve a few typical parcels of them.

One such area is the Yorkshire Dales National Park, which not only has a picturesque and historic landscape with small meadows enclosed with

Superstition demanded that straw dollies should be made and placed in the field so that the harvest would be successful. The craft of making straw dollies soon became aimed at tourism

On the Isle of Mull, in the Western Isles, haystacks are protected from the elements

farm buildings, but also herb-rich hay meadows. The meadows have been used for centuries for grazing and cutting hay. Over a hundred species of plant can occur in the herb-rich meadows, even more than in the surrounding pastures which are encumbered with competitive grasses such as rye-grass and meadow foxtail.

The buttercups of the Yorkshire Dales are the most well-known, but there are other interesting plants growing in the herb-rich meadows including orchids, wood anemone, globeflower, meadow geranium and pignut. During the late 1970s and early 1980s 50 per cent grants were available to farmers to apply nitrogen fertilizer to these meadows, and this had the effect of reducing the plant species found in each square metre by 50 per cent to just fifteen.

It's a topsy-*turfy* world, since the British government in 1991 introduced grants of up to £300 per hectare for farmers and landowners to re-create some of the most attractive English landscape.[5] In all, £13 million has been allocated for this three-year pilot scheme.

Five habitats are targeted for attention: i) chalk and limestone grassland;

ii) lowland heaths; iii) waterside landscape; iv) coastal land; and v) uplands. All of these contain, or should contain, meadows. The grants available are £210 per hectare for replanting chalk and limestone grassland, £225 per hectare for re-creating traditional waterside habitats and for re-creating semi-natural vegetation on coastal land, and £50 per hectare for 'restoration and management of traditional pastures and hay meadows'. It all seems a perfect offer, a golden opportunity, and one wonders how much land will be restored to traditional meadow in all the target areas.

The irony of these 'countryside stewardship' grants is that in some cases the same landscape that was ruined ten years ago is now being re-created, at least as best as landscapers know how. Trying to re-create a harmonious suite of 30–50 species per square metre is fraught with problems, and has never actually been accomplished.

The demise of the British hay meadow has been swift and dramatic this century, and what is present today is a mere 3 per cent of what was originally present in 1930. The latest review of meadow loss in Britain revealed that there were only 5 hay meadows and 1 water meadow remaining in the 322 square kilometres of the Trent Valley in Nottinghamshire, and that only 60 of the 697 hectares of hay meadow surveyed by the then Nature Conservancy Council (now English Nature) in the late 1980s had significant conservation value.[6] In Weardale (County Durham) only 45 of the possible 328 hayfields were of any significant conservation wildlife value.

The point of the recent meadows campaign by the Royal Society for Nature Conservation was to draw attention to the conservation of ancient meadows, some of which exist as 'time-capsules' from another era. In the hills of Wales one such farmstead, a typical example of many, with 4.8 hectares of hay meadows is currently under threat. The farm, Pentwyn Farm in Gwent, has changed little since the 1750s and is nicknamed Little Eden. This was one old farm that Sir David Attenborough sought to bring attention to in the national media in 1991.

Meadows and pastures are disappearing fast near large cities and towns. A recent report on the well-being of London's meadows and pastures revealed a number of interesting sites which have had a traditional role in supporting the city.[7] For instance, both Arrandene Open Space and Featherstone Hills (25 hectares) in the Borough of Barnet, and Horsenden Hills in the Borough of Ealing (82 hectares) were once useful pastures for

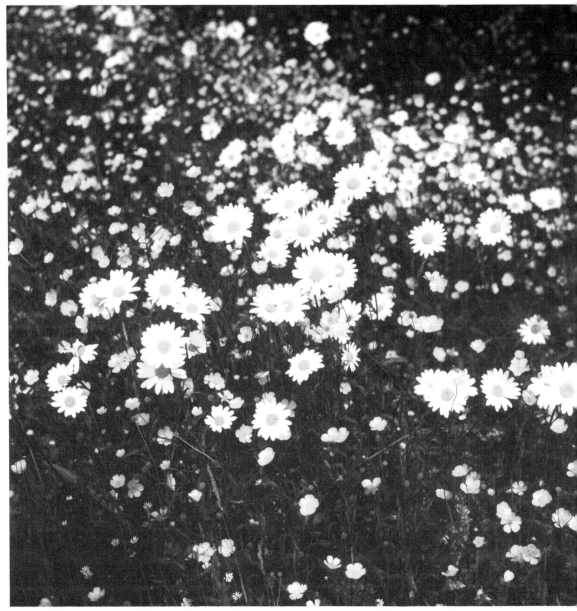

Buttercups, ox-eye daisies, docks and red clover make good partners in this ancient meadow

grazing horses and providing hay for London's working horses. The hill at Horsenden was completely used for hay production at the end of the nineteenth century, but earlier, in 1775 in the region there were 405 hectares of meadow.

The history of London's meadows and pastures, past and present are fascinating and all tied up in the names of places which are still with us, even as reminders; such places as Pippenhall Meadows, Little Britain Grasslands, Fray's Farm Meadows, Moat Mount Fields, Belmont Pasture,

Ravensbourne Meadows, as well as Thamesmead which is now largely built over. Over on the continent, and in the United States, the names of meadows have been borrowed, such as Flushing Meadow, but not always supporting the glorious display of meadow plants which once stood them proud.

Hay meadows support an inordinate number of insects, from plant bugs, grasshoppers and crickets to butterflies and day-flying moths. Of the butterflies, the brown and skipper species are enormously successful since they lay their eggs on various species of grass in the hay meadow. In Europe there are perhaps half a dozen species of skipper likely to be found in a hay meadow, but there are likely to be double or treble this amount in a typical North American one.

North America supports over 250 species of skipper compared to the 50-odd in Europe and they mostly occur in grassy places, some of them in meadows. The possibilities are so much greater for grass-loving insects there since so much of the country is under grass, either as natural meadows, mountain grasslands, taiga, chaparral or prairie – all different types of grassy habitat, some rather drier than others, and each sporting at different times of the year colourful spreads of wild flowers.

Inadvertently transporting butterflies, or their eggs, caterpillars or pupae, is nothing new in the United States. Cutting the hay in one place and transporting it to another has quite naturally (or un-naturally) helped butterflies to exploit new grassy habitats. Such is the case with at least two species, the western skipperling (essentially a skipper by European description), *Oarisma garita*, and the European skipperling, *Thymelicus lineola*, both of which have been moved around via transported hay.[8] It is thought that the occurrence of the western skipperling in the neighbourhood of Lake Huron may have been the result of hay moved from western regions. In the case of the European skipper – an introduced species from Europe in any case – it is believed that eggs were moved in hay and in transported waste from the cleaning of seed of cat's-tail grass within North America.

Introduced species, plants or animals, often prosper where native ones do not. Such is the case with the European skipperling, which has colonized grassy habitats at the rate of 25 kilometres a year since it was introduced into the north-eastern United States in 1910. Despite its incredible success, it has had its pitfalls, since up to twenty-four bodies of these skippers have been found in the slippers of lady's-slipper orchids, a

A tea-party for toddlers in a wild flower meadow. A new generation is introduced to the joys of its – sadly, now all too rare – natural heritage

native species which for some reason does not succeed in attracting the native skippers to its lethal trap.

For butterflies, the hay meadow has a tiered structure, rather like a rain forest. There is the top of the meadow in full sunshine, where the butterfly can partake of rich nectar sources, and there is the interior world of plant stalks and dappled sunlight. On the ground there is another range of wild flowers which might attract the attention of passing butterflies. All areas of this integrated structure are interesting for food, shelter, courtship and mating. Butterflies of this hay meadow world include the meadow brown, hedge brown and ringlet, and the Essex and large skippers. Marbled whites may be common too, and in southern Europe fritillaries and black-veined whites and Bath whites abound in hay meadows. Springtime in flowery meadows can be an exciting time for butterfly observers, and one can even note the antics of courting orange-tips in French meadows.[9]

In Hungary the meadow viper, *Vipera ursinii rakosiensis*, lives in grassy meadowland especially if it is marshy, and on sandy soil, where it feeds on lizards. Although it is a poisonous viper, and has been known to kill children, this meadow viper has a great reluctance to bite.

There are also old reports of otter young resting up in long hay meadow grass and being disturbed by men scything near the river bank. Badgers also use the fields, mostly after the crop has been taken in order to feed on the earthworms which are easier to find in the short stubble. Though badgers much prefer to work pastures than meadows, the fact that they occur here in the presence of grazing cows has led to the unsubstantiated belief that tuberculosis is transmitted between the two animals.

The meadow is full of wildlife either above or below ground. Spiders may be as dense as 300 per square metre, springtails and acarines counted by the thousands per metre, and the turnover of meadow soil through the gut of earthworms per annum over half a hectare is about 10 tonnes, as Darwin carefully worked out.[10] Earthworm numbers are low in improved grassland because of the use of toxic agrochemicals.

There are many people who are re-creating meadows, while there are just as many who are documenting the rapid demise of semi-natural meadows nationwide. Today, in several countries the urge to reinstate the lost meadows of the wayside and countryside, and of earlier times, is particularly strong. One pioneer, on an international front, has been Miriam Rothschild.[11]

Miriam Rothschild was one of the first to attempt to re-create flowering hayfields. She pointed out from the beginning that it was impossible in less than several hundred years to produce a true copy of a medieval meadow, but she proceeded to show that a fair imitation could be obtained in ten to fifteen years. It was important to find a site with a good, natural seedbank, even if the area selected had recently been ploughed and sown with an arable crop. The most appropriate soil was found to be poor with no fertilizers added. On ploughed soil a seed bed was prepared suitable for Timothy grass, and in the autumn sown with a short grass mixture. The following spring, when the grass was growing well, the wildflower seed mixture was drilled in with a John Hunter Rotary Strip Seeder, about 11 kilogrammes to the hectare. The same procedure was followed if the wildflower seed was drilled directly into grass leys, for example an Italian rye-grass hay crop, but in this case the grass was cut as short as possible

Harvesting wildflower seeds at North Meadow, Cricklade

before drilling, and slug pellets scattered behind the drill. Combining was carried out about the third week of July. There is some advantage in cutting and combining half the field somewhat earlier, as some grass seed ripens before others.

The seed mixture collected by combining Sudborough Green Lodge meadow (a flowering hayfield re-created by Peter Nall and Miriam Rothschild's farm manager Syd Jackson thirty-five years ago, and now an SSSI), contains about sixty-five species of wild plants and has been sown by several different trial methods at Ashton Wold. No less than 119 species have been identified in this man-made SSSI!

The most successful 10-hectare fields at Ashton are now excellent imitation 'medieval' hayfields (although lacking the familiar anthills which characterized them before the compulsory ploughing-up ordered in World War II), with a wonderful show of cowslips in the spring. It took about five years before butterflies and moths such as the common blue, small and

Seeds from Cricklade water meadows, where hay has been harvested for at least eight centuries, which are now sold on a commercial basis: 1. Red clover, *Trifolium pratense*; 2. Pepper saxifrage, *Silaum silaus*; 3. Creeping bent, *Agrostis stolonifera*; 4. Great burnet, *Sanguisorba officinalis*; 5. Quaking-grass, *Briza media*; 6. Goat's-beard, *Tragopogon pratensis*; 7. Yellow rattle, *Rhinanthus minor*; 8. Common knapweed (rayed form), *Centaurea nigra*; 9. Ox-eye daisy, *Leucanthemum vulgare*; 10. Ribwort plantain, *Plantago lanceolata*

Nature at its best and under man's continual and long-term management. Here an ancient meadow (Battle, East Sussex) is in full fettle during May. Ox-eye daisy, *Leucanthemum vulgare*, has no particular smell in a meadow, but growers report that it stinks when cultivated *en masse* for seed production

Butterflies

1. Large skipper, *Ochlodes venata*
2. Speckled wood, *Pararge aegeria* (southern form)
3. Southern gatekeeper, *Pyronia cecilia* (male)
4. Meadow brown, *Maniola jurtina* (mating, female on left)
5. Small copper, *Lycaena phlaeus*
6. Long-tailed blue, *Lampides boeticus*
7. Southern small white, *Pieris mannii* (male)
8. Swallowtail, *Papilio machaon* (with larva on fennel stem)
9. Clouded yellow, *Colias croceus*
10. Painted lady, *Cynthia cardui*

Plants

A Lucerne, *Medicago sativa*
B Devil's-bit scabious, *Succisa pratensis*
C Wig knapweed, *Centaurea phrygia*
D Fleabane, *Pulicaria dysenterica*
E Bird's-foot trefoil, *Lotus corniculatus*
F Fennel, *Foeniculum vulgare*
G Wild carrot, *Daucus carota*
H Pennyroyal, *Mentha pulegium*
I Musk thistle, *Carduus nutans*
J Annual meadow-grass, *Poa annua*
K Timothy, *Phleum pratense*
L Agrimony, *Agrimonia eupatoria*

South Western European Butterfly Meadow

The Poppy Field (Les Coquelicots: environs d'Argenteuil), painted by Claude Monet in 1873. Amazingly, scenes similar to this can still be founds in parts of Provence and in the Camargue

Butterflies

1. Common blue, *Polyommatus icarus* (male)
2. Chalkhill blue, *Lysandra coridon* (male)
3. Adonis blue, *Lysandra bellargus* (male)
4. Little or small blue, *Cupido minimus* (male)
5. Silver-washed fritillary, *Argynnis paphia* (male)

Beetles

6. Glow-worm, *Lampyris noctiluca*
7. Two-spot ladybird, *Adalia bipunctata*
8. Green tiger beetle, *Cicindela campestris*
9. Meadow grasshopper, *Chorthippus parallelus*
10. Field cricket, *Gryllus campestris*

Plants

11. Kidney vetch, *Anthyllis vulneraria*
12. Salad burnet, *Sanguisorba minor*
13. Bird's-foot trefoil, *Lotus corniculatus*
14. Dwarf thistle, *Cirsium acaule*
15. Wild parsnip, *Pastinaca sativa*
16. Wild pansy or heart's-ease, *Viola tricolor*
17. Pyramidal orchid, *Anacamptis pyramidalis*
18. Glaucous sedge, *Carex flacca*
19. Dodder, *Cuscuta epithymum*
20. Lichen

A typical meadow scene to be found in downs and dunes

May in the idyllic woods and waysides of Miriam Rothschild's home near Peterborough, Cambridgeshire, where the last of the daffodils and tulips are making way for cowslips

Typical wild flowers of the cornfield are growing here, including corncockle, *Agrostemma githago*, corn poppy, *Papaver rhoeas*, and cornflower, *Centaurea cyanus*

A wild flower meadow growing in a kitchen garden at Emorsgate, Norfolk

A wild flower meadow on Skyline Drive, North Carolina, with Queen Anne's lace or cow parsley, *Anthriscus sylvestris*, coneflowers, *Rudbeckia* sp., and milkweed, *Asclepias*, pushing its way up

A boardwalk through wild flowers, mostly purple loosestrife, *Lythrum salicaria*, and figwort, *Scrophularia nodosa*, both species which enjoy the damp conditions and wet meadows of Norfolk

Corn poppies bring bright contrasting colour to the mellow Gloucestershire stone in this farmyard

A wilder corner of an Irish meadow in the Aran Islands, with alexander, *Smyrnium olustrum*, and Queen Anne's lace or cow parsley, *Anthriscus sylvestris*, and clovers and red campion, *Silene dioica*, in the background

large skipper, meadow brown, ringlet, burnet moth and silver Y began to breed freely in these fields, but they are now abundant. Since these areas are cropped for seed they are cut later than a normal hayfield, thus favouring the survival of early stages of Lepidoptera.

At Ashton Miriam Rothschild spread the hay from one of the best fields on to an adjacent grass meadow and found that this was another effective, if slower, method of adding flowers to the crop. Sika deer proved excellent selective grazers which picked out the grass but tended to ignore broad-leaved plants.

Another unexpected and delightful aspect of these meadows was the appearance of four species of orchid and several other rare plants, such as the dwarf thistle, *Circium acaule*, which were not present in the seed mixture but 'came in from the cold'. Apparently, once the habitat is suitable colonization will proceed quite quickly from the local seed bank.

These experiments in re-creation have shown that wild flowers can be

Ragwort, *Senecio jacobeae*, is a successful meadow species which colonizes areas quickly with its wind-blown seeds. It is, however, hardly the farmer's friend since it poisons cattle when it is eaten undetected in dried hay. Fresh, it is left by cattle, since its poisons are more readily recognized

successfully introduced, not only into hayfields, but along motorways, in parks, recreation grounds and gardens.

Trial and error forms a large part of hay meadow re-establishment, since establishment of plants can be a little fickle and uncertain. Plants do not always perform as they should and there are plenty of unknown factors which plague research. Identical seed mixes can be sown on adjacent plots which share the same results from soil analysis, yet one side will flower, the other will not.

Direct drilling of single species of wild flower such as the ox-eye daisy and buttercup into an already established hay meadow mixture is still being researched. The advantage of this method is that the progress of certain wild plants in invading a field can be accurately judged from the way they work out sideways from their tiny rows.

Hay meadows were always full of wild flowers, and these can sometimes be found around the margins of fields, though less so than ten years ago, even after years of herbicide spraying. The 'herbage strips', as Sir Edward Salisbury called them in 1961,[12] are those areas around fields which have always had a tendency to perform better with wild flowers than areas in the crop itself. Opportunities were always there that did not exist in the depth of the field. This marginal region was brought to everyone's attention in the 1970s when authors would describe the wild flowers of the countryside 'fleeing to edges of the fields'. They were always there, flourishing.

Today, the vanguards of conservation in the agricultural milieu refer to these areas as 'field margins' and there has been deliberate management strategy to widen these field margins so that wildlife will have a better chance of survival. Possible refuges were running out fast. The Game Conservancy, with its prime motive to provide cover for birds and invertebrate food for game birds, came up with very sound ideas for restoring headlands and hedgerows, widening field margins and encouraging farmers not to spray so much. There has been great success with this policy, especially combined with the energies of members of the Farming and Wildlife Advisory Group nationwide.

The harvesting of old hay meadows for their seed makes commercial sense (selling seed is about eight times more profitable than selling hay) and is excellent for nature conservation since wildflower seed is dispersed widely. The method of extraction of the seeds has taxed the ingenuity of operators who have invented all sorts of different types of harvester, some

This model meadow was created with the help of the Farming and Wildlife Advisory Group (Sussex) on a private farm in East Sussex. A corner of a field is an ideal spot for a small meadow

of them looking rather weird with gargantuan tubes stretching out like spider's legs. There are those which suck the ripe seeds from the hay, those that knock it off with a bar set at an exact height, and those which harvest it in a normal manner. The economics of a successful seed harvest are variable, and on less good sites it is easy to make a loss. An average yield from quality old meadows is about 20 kilogrammes per ½ hectare of seed. A wholesale market for the seed must also be found.

Table 4.1 Economics of seed harvesting at Ashton Wold (courtesy of Dr Rothschild)

Harvesting a flowering meadow, Sudborough SSSI, Northamptonshire (35 acres (14.16 hectares)) of permanent grassland, containing 119 wild species of plants; the combined mixture contains 65 species.

	£
Cost of chain harrowing (£3 p.a.)	105.00
Cutting with Massey Ferguson disc grass-cutter (£5 p.a.)	175.00
Making hay, turning once with spider rake (£5 p.a.)	175.00
Combining with John Deere 955 (£25 p.a.)	875.00
Baling with John Deere round baler (£8 p.a.)	280.00
Carting seed to dryer and hay to store, on 10-tonne trailer (£20)	20.00
Seed dressing with Boby grain dresser (two passages) (£200)	200.00
Germination test and identification of species present in seed sample (£200)	200.00
TOTAL EXPENDITURE	2,030.00

Yield

		£
Hay:	40 tonnes at £50 p.t.	2,000.00
Seed:	2 tonnes (after dressing) at £25 per kg	50,000.00
	(NOTE: other catalogue prices for SSSI mixture are £50/kg)	
	TOTAL INCOME	52,000.00

The yield of hay would have been higher if the crop had not been combined.

Once the wildflower seed has been harvested with the special device fitted to the back of the tractor, which carefully flicks the seed from the seed heads, the mass of seed and debris is laid out to dry

NOTE: A 5-acre strip at Ashton was re-sown (in a coarse seed bed) with the seed (combined meadow mixture) from Sudborough at 40 kg to the acre in May 1984. No nitrogen was applied. In July 1985, 6 tonnes of hay per acre were harvested. The bigger yield per acre reflects the difference in soil between Sudborough and Ashton. The same seed mixture cannot be expected to reproduce an exactly similar crop in different areas. Although many of the same species will obviously be present, one may become dominant in one field, and another elsewhere. The hay was found to be equally nutritious as the crops (above average) grown for hay, fertilized and cut earlier. It was tested by ADAS (Cambridge).

There has been some concern about the welfare of the invertebrates inadvertently collected at the same time as the seed, and the latest investigations have centred on Bernwood Meadows nature reserve in Oxfordshire.[13] Meadow browns, *Maniola jurtina*, were looked at in great detail and it was shown that 'somewhat less than 10%' of the total population of the butterflies on the day were removed during harvesting,

Seeds just harvested from a field, drying among the prongs of a Norfolk potato fork, which is used to turn them

most of them dying in the collection procedure. The average density of butterflies in harvested and unharvested areas was 0.045 and 0.062 butterflies in every square metre, demonstrating there had been a decrease. For the meadow brown it was thought that it could sustain this annual removal since it usually has a large population. However its abundance would probably fall. Insect species with much smaller populations were likely to be much more vulnerable to harvesting methods. The fear was expressed that too much seed collection from a field would be detrimental to some insects. Bernwood Meadows was harvested six times in 1987 and three in 1988.

The impact of seed collection from ancient meadows and pastures on the welfare of invertebrates has not been fully investigated. In fact, the work described above appears to have been the only investigation on the subject. Since it was not a comprehensive investigation the conclusion on the impact on invertebrates has to remain open. However, the article does

Table 4.2 Ancient hay meadow seed marketed

Name of ancient meadow	Location	Designation	Supplier
Asham Meads	Otmoor, Oxfordshire	SSSI Grade 1	1, 2
Bernwood Forest nature reserve	Oxfordshire	SSSI	1, 2
Burnt Close	Oundle, Northamptonshire		1
North Meadow	Cricklade, Wiltshire	NNR	1, 2
Oxey Mead	Yarnton, Oxfordshire	SSSI Grade 1	None
Pixie Meads	Otmoor Plain, Oxfordshire	SSSI Grade 1	1, 2
Yarnton Meadow	Yarnton, Oxfordshire	SSSI Grade 1	None
Lampeter Meadows	Dyfed	SSSI	2

Suppliers: 1. John Chambers Wild Flower Seeds, 2. Emorsgate Seeds; for addresses see Further Information, p. 176.

publish recommendations with regard to timing and techniques to minimize the impact on insect populations. It would be a rare farmer, however, who was just as interested in the state of insects as the state of the wild flower fruit heads.

Should it transpire in the future that collecting seed from ancient meadows has a detrimental effect on insect populations, particularly of rare invertebrate species, then English Nature would presumably not hesitate to cease granting licences to people to collect seeds from important Sites of Special Scientific Interest (SSSIs) and National Nature Reserves (NNRs).

One vulnerable species, and a nationally notable one is the forester moth, *Adscita statices*, a delightful green-coloured day-flying moth. Other species likely to be in this category include the grass rivulet, whose caterpillars feed on the yellow rattle, and the small yellow underwing, whose caterpillars feed on mouse-ears, *Cerastium* species.

Paul Waring, who has studied the moths of Bernwood Meadows in Oxfordshire, finds that the prime species of these meadows, the 'jewels in the crown', include the forester, the small yellow underwing, *Panemeria tenebrata*, the blackneck, *Lygephila pastinum*, the emperor moth, *Saturnia pavonia*, and possibly the silver hook moth, *Eustrotia uncula*. He is of the opinion that, 'any management that jeopardises the hordes of night-flying moths of late July or the abundance of larvae on the hedgerows in late May is just as damaging to the natural spectacle that is Bernwood Meadows'.

Lowland meadows in Germany are still reasonably rich in wild flowers, and strip-grazing is commonly used

Open days at wild flower meadows are increasingly important venues on nature conservationists' calendars. Here visitors marvel at a pondside meadow rich in ox-eye daisies and viper's-bugloss, *Echium vulgare*

Table 4.3 Cricklade mixture – a typical mixture of some of the possible 200 species present

Autumn hawkbit	*Leontodon autumnalis*
Bird's-foot trefoil	*Lotus corniculatus*
Black medick	*Medicago lupulina*
Brome, meadow	*Bromus commutatus*
Burnet, great	*Sanguisorba officinalis*
Buttercup, meadow	*Ranunculus acris*
Clover, red	*Trifolium pratense*
Clover, white	*Trifolium repens*
Cock's-foot	*Dactylis glomerata*
Crested dog's-tail	*Cynosurus cristatus*
Daisy, common	*Bellis perennis*
Daisy, ox-eye	*Leucanthemum vulgare*
Dandelion	*Taraxacum officinale*
Fescue, meadow	*Festuca pratensis*
Fescue, red	*Festuca rubra*
Fiorin	*Agrostis stolonifera*
Flax, fairy	*Linum catharticum*
Goat's-beard	*Tragopogon pratensis*
Hair-grass, tufted	*Deschampsia cespitosa*
Knapweed, greater	*Centaurea scabiosa*
Meadow-grass, rough	*Poa trivialis*
Meadow-grass, smooth	*Poa pratensis*
Meadowsweet	*Filipendula ulmaria*
Oat-grass, yellow	*Trisetum flavescens*
Plantain, ribwort	*Plantago lanceolata*
Quaking-grass	*Briza media*
Rye-grass, perennial	*Lolium perenne*
Saxifrage, pepper	*Silaum silaus*
Self-heal	*Prunella vulgaris*
Snake's-head fritillary	*Fritillaria meleagris*
Sorrel, common	*Rumex acetosa*
Vernal-grass, sweet	*Anthoxanthum odoratum*
Yellow rattle	*Rhinanthus minor*
Yorkshire-fog	*Holcus lanatus*

Hay meadows are important habitats for the study of invertebrates, particularly moths, and in his work Paul Waring provides guidance on how to study meadow moths. Altogether 178 species of moth were recorded in the meadows between 1984 and 1986; and over fifty species are known to feed as caterpillars on plants growing in the meadow.

Perhaps one of the most obscure of insects to live in hay meadows is the humble meadow spittle bug which normally lives quite an uneventful life sucking plant juices. Researchers at University of Wales College of Cardiff, have shown that it is an indicator of pollution. It has the uncanny ability to produce dark (melanic) forms in polluted areas. Where the environment is dirty the dark forms thrive, while further away in the cleaner countryside lighter forms survive. The results clearly showed that this little beasty could be used to monitor the relative degree of particulate pollution in an area even in a hay meadow.[14]

Notes

1. Keats, J., 'Over the hill and over the dale'.
2. Ferguson, W.S., Lewis, A.H. and Watson, S.J., 1943.
3. Thompson, F., 1977, p. 50.
4. Pollard, E., Hooper, M.D. and Moore, N.W., 1974.
5. Countryside Commission, *News Release* Ref. NR/91/28, 25 June 1991. This has now been dramatically increased to £38.23m for 1993/4 (Ref. *Countryside*, February 1992, No. 53, p.2).
6. Royal Society for Nature Conservation, 1991, pp. 10–11.
7. Hare, T., 1988.
8. Scott, J.A., 1986, pp. 431, 433.
9. Rothschild, M., 1982, pp. 252–3.
10. Darwin, C., 1974, p. 145.
11. Her father, Charles Rothschild, founded the Society for the Promotion of Nature Conservation (now the Royal Society for Nature Conservation, RSNC). Charles Rothschild obviously had a lot of foresight in making his recommendations of areas of potential nature conservation following his grand tour round England, Scotland and Ireland during which he inspected each site. Some of these sites were later offered protection, while the remainder were not. It would make an interesting study to note the welfare of these sites under the same or different owners and the different regimes of management which have been applied to each of them; there is no doubt that Rothschild's study was both unique and a pioneering work in the history of nature conservation in Britain; see Rothschild, 1987.
12. Salisbury, E., 1961, p. 199.
13. Waring, P., 1988.
14. Lees, D.R. and Steward, J.A., 1987.

CHAPTER 5

DOWNS, DUNES AND COASTAL GRASSLANDS

When meadows laugh with lively green,
And the grasshopper laughs in the merry scene;
When Mary and Susan and Emily,
With their sweet round mouths sing 'Ha,Ha,Ha.'

William Blake, 'Laughing Song'

Probably one of the richest habitats on earth – apart from that of the tropical rainforests – is that which develops on chalk and limestone. And the meadows can be outstanding, with over fifty species of wild flower in every square metre.

The plants which grow on chalk and limestone reflect the nature of the soil type. Technically there is a difference between the two, chalk being a soft powdery material, while limestone is a rocky form of chalk. Both are soluble in water and produce a very alkaline solution. The soil which develops on chalk and limestone is referred to as calcareous, and the plants which live there (and not on clay, for instance) are called calcicoles or chalk-lovers, whereas those plants which hate chalk (and prefer clay, for instance) are called calcifuges, or chalk-haters. Both chalk and limestone are porous, thus providing a light, and very often thin, layer of soil in which the plants live. The plants referred to in this chapter are for the most part calcicoles, those that love chalk.

All habitat types can be defined by the types of plants, and animals, found there. The plants reflect the type of soil, since they are usually very particular as to where they can germinate and survive. In their turn, the species of plants determine the species of animals found in any habitat.

Old Winchester Hill in Hampshire is an important chalk grassland habitat which supports a rich flora and fauna, especially blue butterflies and orchids

There are many insects which are dependent on particular calcicoles as food plants and are thus found nowhere else.

This alkaline quality of the soil reappears in other habitats, particularly coastal ones, whether at Cape Cod in the USA or France's Atlantic dune systems, where sand is derived from crushed sea shells and pounded by the waves into calcareous sand. This has roughly the same pH as chalk and consequently attracts the same range of calcareous species that one might expect to find well inland on chalky sites.

Chalk and limestone occur widely around the world. In England they are found in the Downs of Kent, Sussex and Surrey and in the Cotswolds and Chilterns, and in land on a line stretching from Wiltshire in the south to the north Norfolk coast; and range from the usual white chalk to the unusual reddish chalk mixed with iron to be seen in Norfolk. Scotland has its own very special meadows set on calcareous soil, called *machair*.[1] These areas of machair can be found in the Outer Hebrides in western Scotland

The shepherd and his Old English sheep-dog stand guard over their charges on the rolling Sussex Downs. Shepherds developed a close affinity with nature and relied on the many chalk-loving herbs that grew wild in meadows

and also in the Shetlands. As John Galt (1779–1839) wrote in 'The Canadian Boating Song':

> And we in dreams behold the Hebrides
> Fair these broad meads,
> These hoary woods are grand;
> But we are exiles from our father's land.

Machair is essentially 'dune-pasture' which has developed on flat land covered with wind-blown sand. It may even overlay bog and glacial deposits laid down ten thousand years ago. Machair is often grazed by cattle, sheep and rabbits. Among the flowers which colour the undulating machair are sea pink, clover, plantain and bedstraw. There are lochs in this machair habitat and these can also contain a rich flora including, in one pool, thirteen species of *Potamogeton*, the large group of pond weeds. However, a botanical intruder is currently threatening this diversity of species, and that is butterbur, *Petasites hybridus*, which has become naturalized and is ousting native plants.

Ancient meadows on chalk look like this, with characteristic anthills peppering the landscape. This is on the National Nature Reserve at Ashton Rowant, Oxfordshire, which is particularly rich in chalk-loving flowers and butterflies

In southern England on the chalky Downs and Chilterns much of the original beech, and to a lesser extent yew, juniper and box, was cut down thousands of years ago to make way for open meadows and pastures. The sticky clay of the Weald of southern England was initially too inhospitable to farm when England was first being farmed by man. Sheep-farming was the mainstay of the farmers who used the well-drained downland to fatten their animals. The chalk-loving plants gave the mutton a distinctive flavour, particularly the aromatic herbs such as marjoram and thyme.

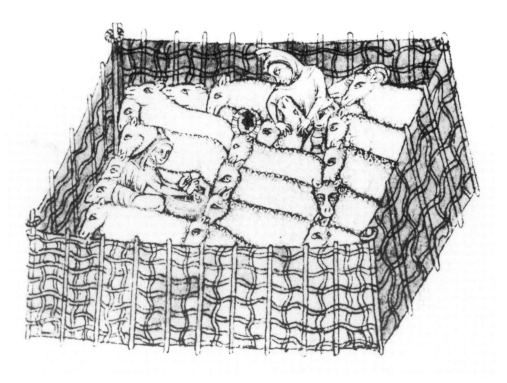

A sheep pen made of hazel wattle is used to constrict the movement of sheep. Here, in this fourteenth-century print, one ewe is being milked, and a ram is being attended by another man. The print is from the *Luttrell Psalter*, dated 1340, from East Anglia

Shepherds then had no resource to the niceties of modern living. They lived off the land, they caught birds and ate them, or sold them – such as the wheatear, once a common bird on the Downs of southern England. They learned to use the wild plants to their own advantage, herbs for flavourings, others for medicine, not only for treating themselves but for treating sick sheep if they were bitten by snakes. While lapwings dropped their wings in pretence to draw attention away from their young, the sheep on these pastures carried on feeding on the nutrient-rich grasses and herbs, and skylarks wheeled through the sky melodiously as the shepherd's keen eye sought their well-concealed nests on the ground.

If today the view of the Downs or Chilterns is of an open well-grazed hilltop, almost bald of any scrub and woodland, it is because it is demonstrating a legacy of the last century and before when there were reputably more sheep in England than people, when there was mass over-grazing of the

Roquefort cheese is an embodiment of the wild flowers of the limestone country in south-west France over which the young sheep – the *brebis* – graze. The typical herbs of southern France are incorporated into the cheese to create its characteristic aristocratic flavour – marjoram, thyme and rosemary

uplands and when there were more open spaces than there are today. The same is true of some major massifs in western Europe which were bald of woodland vegetation at the turn of this century due to excessive over-grazing, but which are now, sadly, covered in monotonous clones of conifers which obscure most of the former pastures and alpine meadows. There are considerable areas of scrub and beech now returning to these chalky areas of downland, although this is sometimes the result of neglect.

In days gone by the scenes from the valley would have been of wattles and the more open hurdles partitioning off large tracts of the Downs into small and temporary fields in which different owners' sheep would have eagerly fed on the chalk-loving plants. Sadly, those days are now gone, but photographs can still recall the integrated life man played with nature in these parts.

In France, the limestone *causses* of the Massif Central are numerous and are plateaux about 1,000 metres high. They have a very sparse, drought-

Typical *causse* habitat in central France, in the Massif of Lozère – in fact, where Robert Louis Stevenson travelled with his donkey – which is rich in wild flowers that enjoy the limestone-rich plateau. Patches of cultivation appear in this stony wasteland, where the flowers are at their best in the spring

Feather grass, *Stipa pennata*, is an attractive wild plant which is common on limestone *causse* in southern France. Best seen against the evening sun, a few hectares of feather grass gently waving in the breeze can be magical

tolerant range of species on them. It is in the *causses* of the *départements* of Gard, Hérault, Tarn and Lozère that the world famous Roquefort cheese is made. The blue veins are the work of a special local fungus, *Penicillin roqueforti*, whose spores are injected into the cheese. In fact the cheese is the embodiment of the range of chalk-loving plants which the sheep (*les brebis*), whose milk the cheese is made from, feed on. At the Roman dining table during the time of Pliny, Roquefort cheese was well thought of, so too at Charlemagne's court.

The Pacific coast of California also has sandy calcareous areas where flowers carpet the desert-like landscape. In fact an Englishman, Captain Vancouver, who sailed along that coast making new navigational charts of the region was astounded by the profusion of colour. Such was the brilliance of wild flowers at certain times of the year that navigators could identify where they were along the coast by taking reliable bearings from them. The coastal area concerned was that part south of Los Angeles towards San Diego, which was then a safe anchorage. The plant species which gave the spectacular display were the California poppy, *Eschcholzia*, rose-coloured sand verbena, *Abronia umbellata*, Indian paintbrush, and wild lupin, *Lupinus*. Padre Crespi was one who noted the flowers, during his perambulations in the region of Los Angeles northwards to the San Fernando Valley in August 1769, as Victoria Padilla describes:

> The valleys and mesas were still vibrant with the orange of the poppy, and the blue of the lupin covered the hills. He was charmed with the lush meadows, the rush-fringed pools (called 'eyes of water' by the Spanish), the lomas covered with Indian paintbrush. He described many of the flowers, the wild grape that clambered over the rocks and trees, and the cactus that offered the padres its purple fruit. . . . Above all, Padre Crespi was enamoured with the wild roses growing in great profusion, for they reminded him of those in Spain. 'Both sides of our way' he notes in his diary, 'were lined with rose bushes of Castile, from which I broke one bunch of six roses opened and about twelve in bud'

and, more amazingly

> Navigators too were thrilled by the coast at a point just west of the Mission San Gabriel, for in spring glowing across the miles to the east was a great carpet of gold. *La Mesa de las Flores* the Spanish called this vast field of poppies covering the area today known as Altadena. So brilliant was the color, it could be seen by ships at sea some thirty-five miles away. It is written that captain set their course by it.[2]

Thirty-five miles is equivalent to the distance from central London to Southend-on-Sea in Essex. Today navigators arriving off the west coast of

Eire in May and June would also be greeted with marvellous sheets of colour, whether off County Kerry, County Clare, the Aran Islands or the Skelligs. Coastal cliffs in this part of Eire are completely covered in sheets of delicate sea pink or, in other places on sand are yellow with the drifts of bird's-foot trefoil.

Table 5.1   Colourful coastal meadow plants in Europe and the USA

Bird's-foot trefoil	*Lotus corniculatus*
Burnet, salad	*Sanguisorba minor*
Chamomile	*Chamaemelum nobile*
Carrot, wild	*Daucus carota*
Evening-primrose	*Oenanthe erythrosepala*
Heath, Cornish	*Erica vagans*
Pink, sea	*Armeria maritima*
Poppy, California	*Eschscholzia californica*
Sea-lavender	*Limonium sinuatum*
Spurge, sea	*Euphorbia paralias*
Stock, sea	*Matthiola sinuata*
Thistle, holy	*Silybum marianum*
Verbena, sand	*Abronia umbellata*
Vetch, kidney	*Anthyllis vulneraria*
Wormwood, sea	*Artemisia absinthium*

England and Wales have numerous coastal meadows among their 4,400 kilometres of cliff coastline, and the Shetland Islands, with their rocky inlets and islands with puffins which nest in the short coastal cliff turf, have 1,610 kilometres of coastline.[3]

In south-west approaches of England the navigator is greeted by the white and pink suffusion of wild carrot and the orange swirls of dodder on the steep coastal meadows of Land's End and on the Lizard peninsula. One plant of particular local note is the Cornish heath which blossoms particularly well in huge impenetrable drifts over the exposed plateau of the Lizard for instance, and which, incidentally, is a great performer in gardens well outside this region. Cornish heath is a threatened, Red Data Book species, which is also found in County Fermanagh, Northern Ireland.[4]

On Tennyson Down in the Isle of Wight the ancient pastures on the

There are few places on earth where one can land on a carpet of flowers, but here, in the Aran Islands off County Clare, the floral reception is a bed of bird's-foot trefoil

rolling Downs are brown, in comparison to the adjacent improved agricultural land which is an 'unnatural' green. This dark and sombre colour is due primarily to one plant, the salad burnet, but interspersed among it are often vigorous spreads of violets, vetches and orchids. On some of these brown Downs are exposed areas of grassland sward which are thought to be some of the oldest exposed meadows in Britain. The prevailing wind has been so consistently strong – straight off the sea – that precious few shrubs have grown and the resultant grassland sward which has developed both on the soil and on flints which litter the slopes contains a range of species found nowhere else. In complete contrast to ancient meadows which have evolved from consistent grazing or harvesting, these downland grasslands (only little fragments can be identified) are the product of the natural environment, not man. This is very unusual. Another delightful meadow experience to be had on the south side of the Isle of Wight is to see rare sea stock, which grows in a precipitous position, side by side with increasingly rare wild cabbage, in the colourful wild grasses at the head of the cliffs.

Wild carrot meadows are common on coastal cliffs, as here on the north Cornwall coast, where the flower exhibits variation in colour from pink to white, and grows as a diminutive sub-species with large umbels

The wildlife diversity and range of species of the Burren in County Clare can hardly be passed over without further elaboration. The Irish meadows here are of extraordinary value in relation to the whole of Britain and Ireland; they are certainly the best place to be floristically during May and early June, and must be one of the key sites in the whole of western Europe.

The Burren flora is remarkable for several reasons: the fact that the region is warmed by the North Atlantic drift (an offshoot of the Gulf

Sheets of kidney vetch, *Anthyllis vulneraria*, smother the cliffs of western Ireland, together with thrift, *Armeria maritima*

Stream); its Lusitanican (southern) connections; its alpine-arctic flowers which are only found here, almost at sea level; and the juxtaposition of plants which love limestone and hate limestone. Nowhere else in Europe are plants such as the spring gentian and the mountain avens found within a few centimetres of the Atlantic's spray. Normally, several thousand metres have to be climbed to see these interesting species – in the Pyrenees or the Alps.

It is also worth mentioning that the vast blue limestone mountains of the

Sea pink or thrift, *Armeria maritima*, makes its own meadow beside the Atlantic on the west coast of Ireland

Burren, which overlook Galway Bay, harbour the Burren orchid or Irish orchid, *Neotinea maculata*, as well as a moth called the Burren green, *Calamia tridens occidentalis*, which is found nowhere else in Europe. The moth was first discovered in the Burren in 1949, and is a regular flier after dark during July and August. In captivity it eats annual meadow-grass, but its food plant in the wild is thought to be blue moor-grass of which there is a lot in the Burren. It is among these colourful Burren meadows that cuckoos rest in groups feeding on the prolific supply of insects, and wheatears find ample shelter among the stones and rocks to construct their nests, bobbing intermittently up and down as they do so, and thus carelessly revealing their secret nest sites.

Further down the coast in the wet meadows of County Kerry the Kerry slug, *Geomalacus maculosus*, is an interesting Lusitanican species found only in this part of western Eire and in Portugal. During the last Ice Age this slug, and several plants, made their way direct from the mountains of south-western Europe via a land bridge. When the English Channel was formed with the rising of the land at the end of the Ice Age, these various

Smothering the limestone rocks as if it were a meadow plant, the mountain avens, *Dryas octopetala*, is an enthusiastic beauty in western Ireland

plants and animals were isolated in their respective places, where, luckily, we can find them today. Their distribution gives us vital clues to previous ecological upheavals.

In complete contrast, on the other side of the Atlantic is another coastal area of great importance. Most people do not realize that the Everglades in Florida lies entirely on a plate of limestone – which is slowly sinking. The water which covers this large expanse is only a few centimetres thick and, like the Camargue in France, makes a wonderful basis for plants and animals to thrive.

On the north-east coast of the United States there is another coastal area which has interesting dune flora. This is Presque Isle,[5] part of a peninsula of 1,190 hectares jutting into the Atlantic. On it have been found five hundred species of plant, including 25 per cent of Pennsylvania's endangered, threatened or rare species. In 1967 Presque Isle was made a National Natural Landmark and it contains such specialities as the hairy puccoon, *Lithospermum caroliniense* – one of the rarest of Pennsylvania's flowering plants, the threatened seaside spurge, *Euphorbia polygonifolia*, and the endangered brook lobelia, *Lobelia kalmii*. Europeans might find it intriguing that silverweed, *Potentilla anserina*, is a threatened species in this part of the western Atlantic, yet on the eastern shores of the Atlantic, in Eire for instance, it is an abundant species, even well inland on the sides of roads.

The fact that there are fifty species of plant per square metre of downland turf is worth more comment. This figure may seem a little far-fetched, even impossible, since on a cursory inspection it does not appear that rich partly because not all plants are in flower at any one time. But there *are* fifty species per square metre if you identify every piece of plant material that you find – even the squinancywort, *Asperula occidentalis*, a tiny recumbent plant nestling in other plants' underbranches.

This great diversity of species is only found on the oldest chalk grassland, especially those that have not been disturbed recently, and ones which are generally referred to by ecologists as 'ancient'. Where the plough has been, or the sweep of the herbicide spray, the number of wild flower species drops alarmingly. Only casuals and common opportunists exploit sites where diversity once flourished. The plight of wild flowers has been repeated a thousand times.

The meadows which developed on established sandy coastal sites around the Mediterranean can be quite exciting. The Camargue can only boast some of the tiniest sand-dunes in the world, barely a metre high, but they sport a colourful springtime assemblage of plants. They are attractive with chamomile, sea wormwood, sea spurges and tall holy thistles. Sometimes the landside part of dunes and wetlands have a violet tinge and this is due to acres of sea-lavender. It is these plants in which the Kentish plover scuttles, and perhaps drops a wing to feign injury so as to draw away attention from its nearly-impossible-to-see young. And it is on these plants that the vocal redshank also seeks to deflect attention from its young.

There is another meadow of sorts in the Camargue, a watery one, which blossoms on the surface of the very shallow freshwater lakes, of which there are fewer and fewer these days because of agricultural improvement. These *étangs* become a sheet of white from the flowers of water crowfoot, all of course replete with enormous numbers of vocal frogs.

The further one gets away from the sea the more vegetation manages to take a hold and become established. The most seaward dunes are affected by salt spray, high levels of wind and the abrasive action of the sand, so that not many plants survive there. Only specialist colonizers sit out the salt spray. A little way landward, other plants grow around the stems of stabilized plants (such as marram grass and sea couch grass) and it is among this group of plants that some of the colourful wild flowers can be found. The dune slacks come alive with the yellow of ragwort, and perhaps drifts of blue viper's-bugloss, or red with glasswort and other acid-loving plants such as the insectivorous sundews. Further landward, grasses and other wild flowers occlude the sand and shrubs such as sea buckthorn become established and the meadow-look disappears.

The great burnet, *Sanguisorba officinalis*, is a strident species, growing up to a metre tall with rich brown flower heads. Often the species grows among lush vegetation, but here it survives on the limestone of the Lizard peninsula in Cornwall

Threats to coastal meadows are enormous in Britain. Demand for scenic coastal positions for caravan sites and tourist developments including golf courses have already eliminated many choice habitats. It is ironic that a lot of the botanical gems occur in the West Country, where increased coastal development has taken place in recent years.

Agriculture has also had a major effect with plenty of damage to meadows in the 1960s to 1980s. Ploughing to the very edge of the cliffs has eliminated some of the finest coastal meadows all over the country. Where there are coastal paths, such as on the north and south coasts of Cornwall, some damage to habitat is inevitable. Invasion of introduced plants, such as the Hottentot fig from South Africa, have also been a nuisance in Cornwall and the Scilly Isles which have significantly warmer weather than elsewhere. The threats continue and pressure on the environment is not likely to abate. Meadows on coastal headlands have a very precarious existence.

Notes

1. Ranwell, D.S., ed., 1977.
2. Padilla, V., 1961, p. 7.
3. Nature Conservancy Council, *Coastal Cliffs and Scarps*, 1982, p. 4.
4. Perring, F.H. and Farrell, L., 1983, p. 33.
5. Anderson, E., 1987, p. 33.

CHAPTER 6

WAYSIDE AND WILDERNESS MEADOWS

When daisies pied and violets blue
And lady-smocks all silver-white
And cuckoo-buds of yellow hue
Do paint the meadows with delight,

William Shakespeare,
Love's Labour's Lost, V. ii. 904

Some of the prettiest meadows that we see as travellers are along waysides and woodland edges. These are linear habitats, long thin drawn-out ones, which always seem to have a rich variety of wildlife. So what makes them special and how extensive are they? Waysides are one aspect dealt with in this chapter; the other is wilderness.

The roadside verge is a formidable place for vegetation, and its sheer energy in productivity, its colour and diversity, gives it equal standing with some semi-natural areas of grassland which support rich meadows.

Old English country lanes were once very much more exciting than they are now; that was before verge-cutting and hedge-cutting, and before lanes and roads were widened thus eliminating the herb-rich roadside verge. The verge was a place for gambolling about, and for geese and chickens to grow fat and scratch about when there were slow and cumbersome haywagons instead of high-speed vehicles. Flora Thompson in *Lark Rise to Candleford* recalled that in her childhood:

The children were allowed to run freely on the grass verges, as wide as a small meadow in places. 'Keep to the grinsard,' their mother would call. 'Don't go on the road. Keep to the grinsard!' and it was many

Four Chinese geese go off to the sodden meadows after a downpour, their silhouettes shiny in the wet mud. Along the wayside, on this February day in Brasted village, Kent in 1960, they would have been able to find adequate forage to feed on

years before Laura realized that that name for the grass verges, in general use there, was a worn survival of the old English 'greensward'.

It was no hardship to her to be obliged to keep to the greensward, for flowers strange to the hamlet soil flourished there, eyebright and harebell, sunset-coloured patches of lady's glove, and succory with vivid blue flowers and stems like black wire.

On the larger roads the roadside verges must have looked particularly cheering for travellers in the spring, since a much larger roadside 'meadow' would have sprung up, especially near water. It is said that the wide verges of the main roads in Britain were so large, and the hedgerows set so far back, so that one had at least a sporting chance of outrunning highway robbers, or at least of seeing them first and preparing oneself before being accosted. The possibilities for floristic meadow verges along these roads would have been great.

English lanes may be quaint in their circuitousness, and are in complete contrast to the straight highways in the United States which provide

This Louisiana meadow, seen here in March, is rich in ragworts – there are sixteen species in this region of North America

wonderful opportunities for plant exploitation. Some wild flowers have made their own colourful stand but in recent years man has also intervened.

The American experience with roadside wild flowers goes back over sixty years and the Texans have really been at the forefront of this general beautification of America's highways. In the early 1930s the women's

---

Table 6.1   Typical roadside wild flowers in the United States

Aster, New England	*Aster novae-anglica*
Bluebonnet, Texan	*Lupinus texensis*
Bluebonnet, yellow rose of Texas	*Lupinus subcarnoscus*
Butterfly weed, milkweed	*Asclepias tuberosa*
Cardinal flower	*Lobelia cardinalis*
Coreopsis	*Calliopsis drummondii*
Evening-primrose, pink	*Oenothera speciosa*
Evening-primrose, yellow	*Oenothera missouriensis*
Everlasting pea	*Lathyrus latifolius*
Goldenrod	*Solidago*, several species
Grass, blue-eyed	*Poa*, various species
Indian blanket, firewheel	*Gaillardia pulchella*
Indian paintbrush	*Castilleja indivisa*
Indian paintbrush, or Scarlet paintbrush	*Castilleja coccinea*
Ironweed, western	*Verononia baldwinii*
Ironweed, yellow	*Verononia alternifolia*
Joe-Pye weed	*Eupatorium maculatum* and *Eupatorium purpureum*
Loosestrife, purple	*Lythrum salicaria*
Marigold, bur	*Bidens*, 13 species
Mint, lemon	*Mentha aquatica*
Ox-eye	*Heliopsis*, several species
Phlox, Drummond	*Phlox drummondii*
Poppy, corn	*Papaver rhoeas*
Poppy, Texas prickly	*Argemone albiflora*
Queen Anne's lace,* (wild carrot)	*Daucus carota*
Ragweed	*Ambrosia mexicana*
Texas star	*Lindheimer texana*
Wild verbena	*Verbena* and *Abronia*, 13 species between them

*   In Britain Queen Anne's lace is another umbellifer called cow parsley, *Anthriscus sylvestris*.

garden clubs of Texas were active in conserving the wild flowers of their roadsides, at a time when the verges were ploughed with mule-drawn mowers. In their turn the public authorities were keen to conserve the verges too, and this led to a statutory mandate not to cut the massed stands of Texan bluebonnets until they had all flowered and set seed. This early conservation law is still in existence today.

It is surprising how many plants are Old World species too, for instance Queen Anne's lace, perennial sweet pea, corn poppy and purple loosestrife. Some of these were introduced from Europe in earliest times. Coreopsis is grown in English gardens, but is a wayside wild flower in the USA, where because of the importance of eliminating ectoparasites from mattresses, it is known by its other common name – tickseed. Hay fever, often attributed to the pollen from goldenrod, is in fact due to the pollen of ragweed.

The Texan enthusiasm for wild flowers has continued to blossom, and the latest supporter has been Lady Bird Johnson, wife of the American President Lyndon B. Johnson. In a magnificent gesture Lady Bird Johnson donated 24 hectares of land in Austin, Texas on the occcasion of her seventieth birthday, so that the National Wildflower Research Centre (NWRC) could be firmly established, and endowed it with a fund of $125,000. The aim of the centre is to conserve and promote the use of native plants in North America, of which there are twenty thousand species, including nearly three thousand at immediate risk of extinction. Through the work of the centre general awareness about wild flowers is promoted and an impressive range of educational leaflets is distributed worldwide.

There is enormous scope for developing the use of wild flowers for landscaping and amenity use in a country with such a large number of native plant species compared with Britain which has a mere two thousand species. The other important attributes of wild flowers are in providing urban colour (colourscaping), and in contributing to agriculture and to medical research. The NWRC has an active research programme which seeks to remedy gaps in general ecological studies of the unresearched flora of the USA.

Texas may have stolen the limelight in promoting wild flowers, but several other states have been equally diligent in conserving their own suite of species. After all, a great awareness of wild flowers is reflected in the

Mrs Lady Bird Johnson has vigorously promoted the use of wild flowers across North America, especially along roadsides and in urban areas

native and indigenous species chosen by various states for their state flowers, or remembered as important species linked to regions – such as the New England aster or the Californian poppy.

Each state in the United States has its own state flower, just as it has its own state tree. And the selection of these wild flowers in fact reflects a tiny part of the meadows likely to be found, or which once flourished. Sadly some of these wild plants have now become scarce. The state flowers are not all natives, red clover and mayflower being introduced meadow plants from Europe. Mayflower is known as lady's-smock or cuckooflower in England.

Table 6.2   State wild flowers

Flower	Latin name	State
Bitterroot	*Lewisia redivia*	Montana
Black-eyed susan	*Rudbekia hirta*	Maryland
Bluebonnet	*Lupinus texensis*	Texas
Clover, red	*Trifolium pratense*	Vermont
Columbine, Rocky mountain	*Aguilegia* sp.	Colorado
Forget-me-not	*Myosotis* sp.	Alaska
Goldenrod	*Solidago* sp.	Kentucky and Nebraska
Hibiscus, yellow	*Hibiscus sinensis*	Hawaii
Iris	*Iris* sp.	Tennessee
Indian paintbrush	*Castilleja* sp.	Wyoming
Lady's-slipper, pink	*Cypripedium acaule*	Minnesota
Mayflower	*Cardamine pratensis*	Massachusetts
Pasqueflower	*Anemone pulsatilla*	South Dakota
Peony	*Paeony* sp.	Indian
Poppy, golden	*Eschscholzia californica*	California
Sunflower	*Helianthus* sp.	Kansas
Violet	*Viola* sp.	New Jersey, and Rhode Island
Violet, native	*Viola* sp.	Illinois
Violet, wood	*Viola riviniana*	Wisconsin

Colouring the roadsides with wild flowers has been a challenge met by many states, from the Louisiana Project Wildflower to Arkansas's Wild-flower Route System which involves forty-six sections of highway which

Giant goldenrod, one of many species which are common along waysides in North America, in the company of knapweeds and native sumachs

have been nominated for special management and conservation, and in which some endangered species occur. There are 'beautification officers' attached to the states of Oklahoma and Florida, North Carolina and Georgia and all have been pioneers in the promotion of wild flowers along roadside verges.

A major advance in the protection of wild flowers of the roadside came in 1987 when a provision of the Federal Highway Act mandated that

Wild flowers create a mini-meadow beside a freeway, with buildings downtown to be seen in the background

25 cents from every $100 (about £50) earmarked for landscape be spent on native plant species. Since 1973 the Federal Highway Administration has been operating 'Operation Wildflower' in league with the National Council of State Garden Clubs and state highway agencies. The Department of Transportation now takes verge management very seriously and sees the economy of converting to wildflower mixes along roadsides. The savings on reducing mowings from seven to two or three times a year make a lot of sense, after the initial start-up fees have been met.

Riding the freeways and interstates of the USA is now a much more colourful experience than ever before thanks to this wild flower enthusiasm, but there are exotic plants to contend with as well. Many exotics have prospered in the hot and humid south, particularly in Florida where Australian pine, water hyacinth and melaleucas have spread seriously, or in Louisiana and Mississippi where kudsu swarms over everything, or wistaria festoons roadside verges, hedges and woods. Some of the exotic roadside escapees are colourful but they tend to be invasive and oust the range of more interesting native species.

There are several places in the USA which seek to conserve the native flora, and among these two gardens are particularly worth mentioning: on the east coast in Delaware, Mt Cuba Centre, the aim of which is to conserve the native flora of the Appalachian Piedmonts, and in California the Santa Ana Botanic Garden, which has an admirable display of wild plants growing in a semi-natural state.

British roadside verges are extensive enough for wildlife. Motorway verges are probably the best roadside habitat for wildlife, and for meadows too, since they are now left completely undisturbed by man who neither walks nor tramples them. With over 10,000 kilometres of motorway in Britain this represents a large linear habitat as a refuge for plants and animals. Of particular note are orchids and cowslips, which have prospered on motorway embankments over the last few decades, much to the appreciation of speeding motorists.

There have always been calls from the bee-keeping lobby to plant up motorway verges with nectar sources for honey-bees, but despite this being a fine idea within limits nothing has been done. Some good nectar sources such as nectar-rich lime trees, however, would not be practicable since this is a forest tree which would grow to 15 metres.

Of far more aesthetic and historic interest is the establishment of English native wild flowers on roadside verges. Miriam Rothschild has promoted this idea in England and has established flourishing colonies of various species on verges of motorways and dual carriageways throughout central and eastern England with her wildflower mixes selected from re-created ancient wild flower meadows.

The vegetation which develops at the side of roads is often very meadow-like, and can encourage strong growth of meadow plants and good populations of insects. Roadsides in Germany are still peppered with the purple-violet of meadow crane's-bill. The M1 motorway north of London was once seeded with Jacob's-ladder, snake's-head fritillary, wild turnip and large bellflower, but these have not taken over from the lank grass. It is on poor, well-drained soils that meadow-like scenes of cowslips, primroses and orchids have developed on English motorway verges. Saltmarsh grasses, more familiar with the salt spray of the coast where their normal habitat is, have now ventured inland along motorway verges, always following the rich salty conditions at the side of the road resulting from regular winter de-icing with salt.

The opportunist ox-eye daisy, *Leucanthemum vulgare*, like the corn poppy, turns up everywhere, even on a newly-developed housing estate on banks of recently-turned soil

Motorway verges are always rich in flora and fauna – since man-the-collector-picker-and-trampler is absent – but in France animals such as foxes, badgers, deer and wild boar, and also the rabbit, owl and squirrel shown on this warning to motorists, can create hazards

In the long lank grass of the roadside verge, sufficient passages are formed to support high populations of small mammals such as mice, shrews and voles. These are hunted by the kestrel, in England, and the buzzard and occasionally the black kite in France. Kestrels and buzzards are frequent sights sitting on roadside posts, the hunt for prey being easy. Black kites used to forage for edible garbage in medieval London, but now they have moved in for easy pickings along the roadsides of France.

Roadside meadows also support an extraordinarily large population of insects, such as grasshoppers, crickets, honey-bees, bumble-bees, butter-flies and moths. Many insects find the rich flora ideal, in fact better than any surrounding kind of habitat (often sterile agricultural or urban land) and expand their populations accordingly. Surprisingly, insects actually benefit from a little pollution: it has been shown that there is more nitrogen in polluted plants and this is passed on to insects which helps them to make new protein and grow. As roadside plants are covered in dust they actually

Rooks, *Corvus frugilegus*, comb the roadside verge for titbits, often hiding them under grass until they are really hungry

Male hedgehogs stomp around their neighbourhood quite a lot, up to 25 hectares, yet females only cover about 10 hectares. Noctunal in their activity, hedgehogs will rummage through meadows, especially wild urban ones

grow faster since the internal temperature of the leaf is increased – just like being in a greenhouse. The increased productivity of the plant leaf is all good food for hungry caterpillars which then grow more quickly. So a little pollution is not bad. Insects, like plants, do get nasty pollutants such as heavy metals, zinc, lead, cadmium and mercury incorporated into their tissues, but they seem not to be too much inconvenienced by it.

Wild flower seed may fall off the backs of trucks and juggernauts – coriander from the Mediterranean is a favourite example – but the high-speed vehicles probably also have some beneficial effect in whistling ripe seed from one place along the verge to another further up. Wild flower seed has its own potent means of dispersal, even from continent to continent, but it has always been aided by man. Transport and traffic have always played a key role. The native, or indigenous, species of any country always have to contend with introduced alien species, such as Canadian fleabane, *Conyza* canadensis, and these more often than not oust some of the native flora. This is because they are not restrained by the local impediments such as pests, disease and local climate.

To take Britain as an example, up to 30 per cent of its plant species are introduced. And the nearest place for many interesting introduced species to come from is the Mediterranean – a mere 1,127 kilometres away to the south-east. The Mediterranean area was always a favourite for Englishmen on their grand tour of Europe, and among them there were plenty who collected all sorts of sundry seeds. Sea and overland trade helped to bring in many a Mediterranean plant species too. The importation of wool to Scotland and the Shetlands, the seeds cleaned from the wool (collectively called shoddy) being discarded into the countryside where they germinated and prospered, also had a dramatic effect. In his book on grasses, Hubbard[1] states that there are 160 species of indigenous or naturalized grasses in Britain, and another 200 species introduced via the sheep trade as shoddy.

It is perhaps apocryphal that the Romans were responsible for introducing wild flower seed throughout Britain, and perhaps to Britain, through seeds which became trapped in the leather thongs of their shoes and in other apparel being released somewhere later upon a Roman road. Mediterranean plants then prospered along the wayside. On military campaigns horses and pack animals had to be fed with hay, sometimes carried as stores over several hundred kilometres alongside the armies. It is perhaps also apocryphal that cannabis grows at those 'reserved for police

Regular maintenance of roadside verges by seasonal cutting is ideal for meadow creation – it has the same effect as grazing

vehicles only' places on motorways, as a result of cannabis seeds falling out of the pockets of officers who have previously been at the scene of a drugs haul. Perhaps a grain of truth somewhere: it only needs one grain.

It is thought that the mounted Cossacks brought species such as the warty cabbage, *Bunias orientialis*, from southern Russia to western Europe following the Napoleonic Wars.[2] Sieges also did a lot to introduce alien meadow plants. In the siege of Paris during the Franco–Prussian War, for

The finger-grasses are easy to recognize with their finger-like parts of the flower, and occupy the edges of meadows in southern Europe. This one is *Digitaria sanguinalis*

instance, a variety of grasses and leguminous plants blossomed around the soldiers – a siege flora, or *flora obsidionalis*, which originated from hay brought from southern France and Algeria. Ships plying between the Mediterranean and Britain carried sand as ballast which also contained alien seeds. The movement of grain also contributed a major route for seeds, and it is reported that as early as 1762 exotic plants were growing around Montpellier in southern France. In fact, about five hundred exotic species or wool adventives had been recorded from around one particular mill at

Port Juvenal. Another way that wild flower seed was introduced through Europe was via fruit which was packed with hay from meadows along the Mediterranean coast to prevent frost damage. These included:

Table 6.3 Mediterranean hay seeds distributed in Europe

Cress, lesser swine	*Coronopus didymus*
Fescue, rat's-tail	*Vulpia myuros*
Fumitory, dense-flowered	*Fumaria densiflora*
Grass, black	*Alopecurus myosuroides*
Kochia	*Kochia scoparia*
Medick, toothed	*Medicago polymorpha*
Mignonette, wild	*Reseda lutea*
Mustard, hare's-ear	*Conringia orientalis*
Plantain	*Plantago lagopus*
Rupturewort, hairy	*Hernarian hirsuta*
Vetch, bithynian	*Vicia bithynica*
Yellow-sorrel, procumbent	*Oxalis corniculata*

Travelling gypsies also helped to spread the thorn apple, *Datura stramonium*, a medicinal plant which helps remedy breathing problems, and a spurge called *Euphorbia uralensis* from southern Europe and western Asia to Europe.[3] Spurge contains poisonous alkaloids but a small concentration of a poison is often efficacious for treating ailments.

As people increasingly found the world a smaller place, fewer places remained beyond the effects of man. Wildernesses and their meadows, were appreciated by ecologists and naturalists – for instance, by one of the pioneers of the New World, John Muir ('America's apostle of wilderness', 1833–1914) who, earlier this century, helped to press for preservation of nature's choicest pieces. Muir was raised in Wisconsin and tried to buy out his brother's share of the family farmstead. He wrote to him, 'sell me the forty acres of lake meadow, and keep it fenced, and never allow cattle or hogs to break into it . . . I want to keep it untrampled for the sake of its ferns and flowers'.[4]

Muir never raised enough money to buy his brother out, or to have his own meadow, but he was able to use all his energies to try to conserve much of America's prize habitats, which included meadows, especially Alpine ones. National parks and wilderness areas are not always safe today

Earlier this century the Suffolk countryside blazed with the carpets of pyrethrum flowers – actually a species of chrysanthemum – which used to be grown as a source of derris dust, a useful insecticide which is non-toxic to man. Here at Long Melford the flower heads are being gathered at the start of the pyrethrum harvest

from development, especially for oil, and there have been many potential threats from man.

One wilderness area currently under grave threat is the Arctic National Wildlife Refuge in north-east Alaska. This barren area of 8 million hectares is populated by two groups of ethnic Indians, Gwich'in Indians, or Caribou People, of the south and Inupiat Indians, or the North Slope Indians, 644 kilometres to the north. The United States government wishes to extract oil from this tundra area. Proposals to carry out offshore drilling riles the Inupiats since they own coastal areas and are dependent on seals, and plans to take oil from the southern part riles the Gwich'in Indians since their culture is dependent on their 180,000 herd of caribou.[5] The caribou of course are dependent upon the tundra habitat which supplies suitable calving grounds and summer food, in the form of prolific wild flowers. It remains to be seen how this intrusion into the way of life of the

Indians and the destruction of much of the habitat will affect the ambience of this lovely area which was originally conserved for the public good. All this in an area not too far from where the tanker *Valdez* released its load of oil. Words can hardly sum up the beauty of this part of the world, but one biologist described its communities as having a 'charismatic megafauna', implying that its flora and fauna were one of the most attractive suites to be found in nature.

'Wilderness' is not usually used to refer to British habitats, though in a very loose manner the term has been applied to some parts of Scotland. One such area which made the news in 1991, since it was up for sale, was Mar Lodge in the Highlands – some 3,112 hectares. It is reputed to be one of the most important wilderness areas in western Europe, and contains some remnants of the ancient Caledonian scots pine forest. Many of the British National Parks contain rich grasslands and open meadow-like glades in woodlands.

In the USA one city – Portland in Oregon – using the latest technology investigated what habitats it had left worth preserving. It had a shock, for in comparing the six hundred infrared aerial photographs it took of upland meadows, coniferous forests and wetlands in 1989 with an inspection in 1990, it found that 10 per cent of these open spaces had disappeared under the bulldozer. What is true for Portland is probably true for a great many American cities and towns which are still experiencing surges in urban development and colonization of green field sites. In the Portland area there are regional 'megafauna' Greenspaces campaigns, and elsewhere in the USA there are other open area groups such as Open Space America, established in 1990, and the Trust for Public Land based in San Francisco, which was established in 1972. To date, the latter has saved more than 202,500 hectares.

One of the beauties of wilderness areas are their butterflies. There are an enormous number of fritillary species in North America, and the wide open grassy prairies have given much scope for their evolution and diversity there. The meadow fritillary is a common sight in the grassy plains where there are wild flowers. There are at least two fritillaries which show a distribution relating to the last Ice Age. These are the relic meadow fritillary, *Boloria kriemhild*, and the uncompaghre fritillary, *Clossiana acrocnema*, the latter only first discovered in 1978 at 4,000–4,250 metres in the Colorado mountains. It became isolated in the mountains after the

Sheets of wild flowers bloomed across America before Westerners arrived. The wild flowers of the prairie, coastal habitats and grasslands were always rich and in recent years there has been much enthusiasm in restoration ecology allowing native species like coreopsis to take over again

melting of the ice, and evolved from its close relative the dingy Arctic fritillary. The relic meadow butterfly is curiously found in Idaho and Utah. Stretching down into Mexico is the western seep fritillary, *Speyeria nokomis*, which is named after the watery habitat in which it may be found – seeps and meadows and canyon bottoms.

Colourful fritillaries are some of the larger and more attractive butterflies of arctic meadows, but there are numerous other species belonging to the skipper family. Some people do not regard skippers as butterflies, since they have several affinities of moths. But in North America there are well over 250 species of skipper, which is quite staggering. Compare this to the handful of skippers in Europe. It is living proof that the North American skippers have exploited the vast grassy areas, – prairies, natural grasslands, meadows, canyons and chaparral – which exist over much of the central, southern and western United States, as well as further north and west in Canada. Skippers have been more successful in meadows than fritillaries for sheer number of species.

Table 6.4 Meadow plants by meadow names

Those listed are species referred to as 'meadow' plants, or with their second latin name as *pratensis* or *pratense* from the latin *pratum* meaning meadow. The list includes species found in Europe as well as North America. Some give important structure to meadows and pastures and have travelled the world, involuntarily or especially to give new life to new pastures. Others are simply colourful additions to meadows.

Flower	Latin name	Note
Meadow beauty	*Rhexia lutea*	North American, 10 native species.
Meadowbright	*Caltha palustris*	European native, usually called marsh-marigold in Britain, but once called meadowbright in Northamptonshire.
Meadow brome	*Bromus commutatus*	
Meadow buttercup	*Ranunculus* species	General term for several European native species.
Meadow clary	*Salvia pratensis*	European native, clary is a corruption of 'clear eyes' since the seeds of meadow clary were put in water to swell up, then they were put in the eye so that any foreign body would stick to the mucilage which surrounded the seeds.
Meadow crane's-bill	*Geranium pratense*	European native, a colourful species in old meadows.
Meadow crowfoot	*Ranunculus* species	European native, several species of which live in shallow water.
Meadow foam	*Limnanthes* species	North American, six species native to the west coast; do not occur in meadows in Europe, only found in gardens as an effective ground cover and usually called foamflower or poached-egg plant.
Meadow-grass, alpine★	*Poa alpina*	Found principally in the arctic regions of Europe, Asia and North America,

127

Flower	Latin name	Note
		and known in North America as alpine blue-grass.
Meadow-grass, annual★	*Poa annua*	
Meadow-grass, Balfour's★	*Poa balfouri*	
Meadow-grass, broad-leaved★	*Poa chaixii*	Introduced into North America and also known as chaix's meadow-grass.
Meadow-grass, bulbous★	*Poa bulbosa*	Introduced to North America.
Meadow-grass, early★	*Poa infirma*	
Meadow-grass, flattened★	*Poa compressa*	Introduced into North America and known as Canadian blue-grass. In Canada it is useful as a pasture grass on poor dry soils.
Meadow-grass, glaucous★	*Poa glauca*	
Meadow-grass, narrow-leaved★	*Poa angustifolia*	
Meadow-grass, rough★	*Poa trivialis*	Introduced into North America and also known as rough blue-grass.
Meadow-grass, smooth★	*Poa pratensis*	Introduced into North America and also known as Kentucky blue-grass.
Meadow-grass, spreading★	*Poa subcaerulea*	
Meadow-grass, swamp★	*Poa palustris*	Introduced into North America in about 1814 as a grazing or hay plant, and is also known as fowl blue-grass.
Meadow-grass, wavy★	*Poa flexuosa*	
Meadow-grass, wood★	*Poa nemoralis*	Found in Europe, North America and Asia, and also called wood blue-grass.
Meadow kerses, or flower	*Cardamine pratensis*	Usually known as cuckoo-flower or milk-maid.
Meadow pink	*Lychnis flos-cuculi*	More usually called ragged-robin, this plant is disappearing fast from meadows that are drained.

Flower	Latin name	Note
Meadow rocket, Meadow orchid	*Orchis incarnata*	Also called marsh rocket, an old name for it in Dumfries and Galleway.
Meadow-rue	*Thalictrum flavum*	There are 10 species of meadow-rue in European meadows.
Meadow saffron	*Colchicum autumnale*	Also called naked lady since the pink flowers burst forth from the ground without having any greenery around them.
Meadowsweet, Meadow maid	*Filipendula ulmaria*	Once belonged to the *Spiraea* genus, and has been investigated for its 'aspirin' qualities. It is a typical species of wet meadows.
Meadow saxifrage	*Saxifraga granulata*	Found in Europe on basic and neutral grassland.
Meadow vetchling	*Lathyrus pratensis*	

★ Many species of these 'meadow grasses' (most native to Europe) are known. The best treatment of meadow grasses is in Hubbard's classic book, on *Grasses*.

The American prairie is a vast part of middle and mid-west America which is essentially a very grassy area. The word comes from the French for a 'meadow-tract'. The prairies spread from southern Michigan, western Ohio and Illinois (known as the Prairie state) westwards to the foothills of the Rocky Mountains, including Indiana, Missouri, Iowa, Wisconsin and Minnesota. This is a distance of some 2,415 kilometres. In Canada the prairies run from Winnipeg to the Rockies.

There are 32 million hectares of National Park in the United States, and about 50 per cent is designated as wilderness. Much of the wilderness was prairie and the term 'prairie-schooner' referred to the vast sea of grass that the first colonists witnessed – they could see further than man could journey in a day.

Much of the early wilderness disappeared due to the 'felling ax, the crosscut saw, barbed wire, Sharp's carbine, the Winchester Repeater' and 'John Deere's sod-breaking steel plow . . . that could rip the ancient root tangles of giant bluestem turf and flip it into long black furrows'.[6] John Deere's 'Prairie Queen' plough came into use in the 1850s and was responsible for much of the loss of meadows and natural pastures. For the early colonists with their honeybees, the honey crop was prodigious from the natural expanse of wild flowers. At the turn of the nineteenth century the sound of honeybees was new to the native Indians – and they knew that if they saw 'white-man's flies' the white-man was not far behind. The large honey crops were stored in hollow cottonwood tree trunks, cottonwood being a readily available riverside tree.

The prairie has its lush meadows, gulches and foothills, but it is essentially a dry grassy plain, undulating and without trees. It is quite likely that the Indians contributed to the cutting down of a significant number of the trees and introduced more grassland, but it is also likely that much natural prairie occurred before Indians exploited the land. The buffalo is a natural grassland animal which depended on this open habitat for its food and way of life, and its huge herds travelled the prairie until slaughtered by the waves of white men moving west over the new country of America. Now the buffalo is making a comeback in those areas set aside for its conservation. The Indians knew how best to live with buffalo without decreasing their numbers significantly.

There is great variety in the number of plant species that occur on America's prairies. In Texas there may be as many as two hundred species of different types of animal in 250 hectares, while to the north there may be only fifty species since there it is much more cold and austere. The number of animals which exploit the grass habitat are legion, from butterflies such as the skippers and the ringlet butterflies which lay their eggs on grasses, to the prairie chicken – a type of grouse – and the prairie dog, – a social mammal which lived in subterranean 'cities' which ran for several kilometres and contained many thousands of individuals although these have mostly been destroyed now. The prairies are also home to rattlesnakes, burrowing owls and tarantulas, as well as prairie moles, prairie squirrels, prairie hawks and prairie warblers.

American prairie may in some cases be wilderness where man, particularly Indians, has not interfered with the habitat. In Europe there is little wilderness, but there is a lot of open grassy wilderness in both the United States and Canada, and much of it is now accessible in preserved areas for tourists to enjoy. To qualify as wilderness, the habitat, or suite of habitats,

Establishing a wild flower meadow in North America

When trying to establish a wild flower meadow in North America it is essential to note the type of habitat the wild flowers are used to. The problem is complicated by the vastness of the country and the range of habitats in which wild flowers are found. One needs to be precise about which suite of flowers one proposes to establish since there are eight major grassland habitats:

Bunch-grass desert shrub	Mixed grass prairie
California grassland	Sagebrush grassland
Coastal prairie	Short-grass prairie
Eastern prairie edge	Tall-grass prairie

All but sagebrush and the California grasslands are to the east of the Rocky Mountains and so receive limited amounts of water, which is ideal for grasses. One of the most colourful of natural habitats for striking wild flower meadows is the tall-grass prairie, which extends from Oklahoma in the south and continues through Minnesota and into southern Canada.

Establishing a wild flower meadow can be fun, but it is necessary to keep a strict eye on various environmental parameters. The meadow must be in full sunshine so that the plants will flower, fruit and disperse their seeds effectively. Establishing a meadow in the shadow of a tree or along a wall will not be successful. There must be adequate amounts of air to circulate through the meadow and to prevent mildew and other deleterious fungi-rotting plants and fruits. And the meadow must be on the flat or on gently undulating ground so that there will be no erosion of precious soil. As a general rule, the soil into which meadow seeds are sown should be fairly nutrient-poor, though this does depend on which type of meadow is being established. One can imagine a floriforous meadow in the mountains with dark rich humus soil and which is also fairly squelchy. The home meadow should also have a high moisture content. The imaginary meadow in the mountains, which is so often seen, also has long grass whose well-dispersed stems are well-separated (i.e. it is not a green lush meadow). The spaces between the stems are perfectly ideal for large butterflies to fly between, i.e. below the canopy of the meadow. This openness is a feature which is perhaps hard to emulate in the garden, but is an ideal to work towards.

has to be not only extensive but it has not to have been subject to intensive human use. Some wildernesses have natural grassy areas, with tundra, taiga, or prairie, and it is in these sorts of habitats that colourful meadows with excitingly coloured plants, and insects abound.

In Europe, perhaps the best, or the most appropriate, example of a prairie animal would be the pratincole, since its name – from the latin *pratum*, a meadow, and *cole*, an inhabitant – demonstrates very nicely its close link with the grassy habitat. There are two pratincole species (the collared and the black-winged) in southern Europe, and it is always a delight to find a group of them sitting in the open, looking rather like overgrown swallows with long wings. Of course, the important prairie-like stony ground to the east of the Camargue in southern France known as La Crau (a place which has been somewhat degraded in the last few years, like the rest of the Camargue[7]) used to be a fine place to see pratincoles. Other birds of the flat stony, sometimes grassy, expanses are the bustards, of which there are four species in Europe, some of them living in sparse desert, but nearly always preferring to run rather than fly when danger threatens. Their brown grass-like camouflage serves them well in the absence of any cover. They have diminished in numbers just like the stone curlew, *Burhinus oedicnemus*, which was once widespread in Europe. This species is also a speciality in the stony Breckland of East Anglia in Britain.

Notes

1. Hubbard, J., 1968, pp. 12–13.
2. Castri, di F., Hansen, A.J., and Debussche, M., 1990, pp. 38–9.
3. Ibid.
4. Arden, H., 1973, pp. 433–58.
5. Eathorne, R., 1991, pp. 34–5.
6. National Geographic Society, 1973.
7. Feltwell, J., 1990, pp. 16–17.

CHAPTER 7

GLADES

Evidently there was such a thing as woodland grassland in prehistory,
probably in the form of small glades where grazing was specially
concentrated.

Oliver Rackham, 1988[1]

Woodland glades as defined here are small areas in woodland which burgeon with wild flowers. They are not necessarily 'permanent glades', which some experts, such as Oliver Rackham regard as being at least 500 years old, though there is some overlap.

The glades here are those that are often found in woods, or hacked out of overgrown woods by conservationists. They are percolated with light, vibrant with wild flowers and full of insects. Apart from the permanent glades, there are many glades which are transitory due to the natural phenomenal ecological forces of growth, competition and colonization. To capture the allure of the woodland glade, which is rather like a meadow, is the point of this chapter. The mystical, enchanting woodland glade, which is alive with insects silhouetted in the clear light that imbues the area, is never exactly the same when visited again. A change in time, space and energy takes place and the ethereal and aesthetic ambience moves on, perhaps to something better, but always to a more mature stage, from meadow to light woodland.

Glades were sometimes continuous with the rides and forest margins where certain plants grew, as Oliver Rackham says:

we do find, at low altitudes throughout prehistory, occasional pollen grains of fruits of what I call 'woodland grassland plants' such as cuckooflower, devil's bit and bugle . . . These do not flower in shade, but are now characteristic of woodland edges and rides.[1]

Ancient deer parks are sometimes good sites for old pastures, especially those which were enclosed by the Normans after the Conquest in 1066. Relic fauna, such as some beetles, are now only found in these old pastures, thus representing pre-1066 fauna

The woodland meadow represents a transitory stage in the cycle from an open habitat to a wooded habitat. As seedlings and scrub grow up, the glade is shaded-out and is eventually absorbed as part of the main wood. Meadow species which survived in the glade cease to exist but may spring up elsewhere nearby in another glade. The ability of plants, and, for that matter, animals to move around depends upon man managing the woodlands with the kind of small-scale felling treatment that used to be

A pugnacious butterfly, the large skipper, *Ochlodes venatus*, spends a lot of time sunbathing, only sallying forth to attack other butterflies and insects which enter its territorial airspace

typical up to a hundred years ago, the distance between each block of woodland not being too far, thus enabling seeds and insects to disperse easily. Sadly, today's economics dictate that discrete parcels of woodland cannot be so treated. And when neglected coppice woodland is felled, it is often in extremely large parcels, which is of no use to wildlife since it cannot colonize between similar areas so widely dispersed.

The marvel is that meadows should be in woodland at all. These precious parcels make up the patchwork of woodland and glade which is typical of several types of woods in Britain and Europe. Wherever trees fall down because of storm, disease or man, the space left becomes a meadow. It is as if the ground is then able to unleash the genetic material held in the seeds locked up in the soil – which is in fact exactly what happens. The dormant seeds ticking over in the lower levels of the soil are just waiting for this moment to be brought to the surface, perhaps one hundred or two hundred years after they first came to rest in the ground, when the warmth

A typical German lime wood with an understorey of cuckooflower, *Cardamine pratensis*

of the sunlight and the moistening nature of the falling rain helps them to germinate. The fresh soil is then immediately colonized by the sprouting seeds of local plant species and, of course, by alien plants which often do better. The effect is a flush of colour the following spring, or, in the case of biennials, such as the foxglove or mullein, the spring after that.

There are all sorts of woodland glades or clearings which qualify as meadows, including those sparser areas in light woodland which look tempting and attractive as one marches through a wood. Silver birch woods in the spring can be a spectacle with a green carpet studded with wild flowers before the trees' green leaves have unfurled. There are also those woodland glades which one discoveres by accident in much thicker woods. Where the forester or woodman has been, he frequently leaves a small plot on which he has had his fires for brushwood. These areas are very slow to colonize and they therefore grow up as light areas within an ever-encroaching woodland. The orange glow of mosses here can be

Dandelions proliferate and make a wonderful show in grassy meadows, especially orchards

outstanding. Then there are those mossy delights nestling in rather soggy parts of the wood where ordinary woodland species cannot survive. The squelchy ground is colonized by carpets of green moss which catch the sunlight and give the interior of the wood a verdant look. Of particular note here are the orange–yellow *Sphagnum* mosses which form a rich pile, and a delightful feathery moss which is finely divided like tamarisk, its name reflecting this pleasant nature, *Thuidium tamariscinum*. Some specimens stand so proud of the floor that they look like ferns.

The wood or forest can be so thick and its vegetation so intermingled that the clearing is a bright surprise in an otherwise dark habitat. These are similar in nature to rainforest clearings where tumultuous challenges between lianes, ferns, trees and ground plants constantly surge to close the sunny gap. A rainforest clearing is not that far removed from a temperate woodland glade in the northern hemisphere. The colour from opportunist plants is just as exciting, and the sense of change just as urgent.

To the eyes of the English a bluebell, *Hyacinthoides non-scriptus,*[2] wood is rather like a woodland with a meadow in it. The ground is often shrouded in blue in April and May before the complete leaf canopy of the oak has had a chance to completely unfurl and cut out most of incident light. This is just after the primroses and the similarly-coloured brimstone butterflies are out in the woods and clearings.

Where clearings occur, the bluebell does much better, carpeting the ground with a sturdier growth of plants, and providing a deeper, firmer shade of blue, as if growing conditions in these woodland meadows was much better than in the pallid interior of the wood. The fact is that conditions are better for growth in strong sun, but the catch is that the bluebell cannot possibly always sustain this enhanced rate of growth and ebullience. It is obliged to be a shade-loving plant, for it cannot sustain

Bluebell, *Hyacinthoides non-scriptus*

growth in the open when in competition with plants which thrive better in direct light. There are exceptions, and one open site is near Cheddar in Somerset, where bluebells show a wonderful spread in hay meadows.

In woodland which has been grubbed of its trees, the bluebell carpet can be outstanding in the first spring, but it will start to degenerate after the second year in favour of more competitive plants. For a plant which delights in the shade of woodlands it is extremely successful, not only reproducing by its prolific seeds, but also by its bulbs. The tragedy in moving bluebells from the sanctuary of their woodland retreats to the glory of the garden (which people often do, despite it being illegal) is that the plants always die, since the garden is normally too sunny a place.

The bluebell is not the only successful plant to be found in the woodland glade. In slightly wetter places than the bluebell can bear, the woods become alive with the foamy flowers of wild garlic. Sometimes there is a relatively straight line between bluebells and the wild garlic marking this wetter interface, and the wild garlic grows down to the edge of the sticky clay at the water's edge if there is a woodland stream. As far as natural monocultures go, bluebell and wild garlic are one of the most effective.

Windflowers, or wood anemones, *Anemone nemorosa*, can make an eye-catching stand in woods and clearings as well, in much drier areas often on sandy soil which support light woodland such as silver birch. Wood anemones bring up their bright heads early in the year in time for the hibernating insects to come out to imbibe nectar and to pollinate them. And bobbing around on the fresh spring winds they do earn their name of windflowers.

Dog's mercury, *Mercuralis perennis*, has had more than its fair share of limelight in recent years than the other one hundred or so indicator species which botanists use to date the age of a wood.[3] It is a woodland species which carpets clearings with its green mantle, existing in two sexual forms with swathes of single-sex plants – as undistinguished as they are with their little pom-poms (female) and tassles (male). An ecologist's classic plant, the dog's mercury (which is not particularly poisonous to dogs) co-exists with other woodland glade plants which attract insects, so the glade is not altogether bereft of colour or insects and attendant birds; its seeds are like little balls of mercury. Far more interesting is its sometime associate, the tiny town hall clock, *Adoxa moschatellina*, or indeed the upstanding, green-flowered, spurge laurel, *Daphne laureola*.

Rampant ramsons or wild garlic, *Allium ursinum*, may give an overpowering smell of garlic to the woods, and all areas downwind, but it produces a monoculture of colour in woodlands where it is a little too wet for bluebells

Forestry rides offer an ideal opportunity for wildlife to hang on in old habitats destroyed and then forested. Where these ancient sites have been converted to forestry, there is the opportunity for the original suite of species to re-establish itself along the access rides laid out like gridwork through the forests. This is not only good for plants and their dispersal, but for the dispersal of the more mobile butterflies, such as some of the woodland fritillaries. The fact that the rides join up and lead to other adjacent sites means there is at least some continuity in the neighbourhood.

Typical flowers found in glades: top left, wood anemone, *Anemone nemorosa*; bottom left, snowdrop, *Galathus nivalis*; top right, daffodil, *Narcissus pseudonarcissus*; and bottom right, St John's-wort, *Hypericum perforatum*

As George Peterken said, 'a modern paradox is that the richest "unimproved" grassland is often to be found in woodland'.[4]

The forestry ride or woodland clearing may also be comprised of a rocky area or a very wet area where trees cannot establish themselves. Here a grassy habitat can prevail, and a sort of woodland meadow complete with wild flowers and butterflies can live deep in the wood.

A relatively new conservation body in London, Plantlife, has recently collated the results from a number of experts about the effects of changing climate on wild flowers, and on bluebell woods in particular. The results are alarming since it is suggested that the unique bluebell wood is under threat because of global warming. Bluebells rely upon the cool spring air to grow successfully into the rank vegetation that is typical. With slightly increased temperatures other plant species which prefer the warmer weather are likely to smother the bluebells and degrade the sheets of bluebells with which so many are familiar. The fabulous blue woods of spring may be on the wane.

Silver-washed fritillary, *Argynnis aglaja*

There are other species too which are likely to be affected by the changing weather: wood anemone, *Anemone nemorosa*, valerian, *Valeriana officinalis*, and the much rarer grass-of-Parnassus, *Parnassia palustris*. The presently more northern species in Britain, such as the nationally rare Jacob's-ladder, *Polemonium caeruleum*, the mossy saxifrage, *Saxifraga hypnoides*, and various mosses and liverworts are likely to decline with increased temperatures, in favour of Mediterranean species which may infiltrate the southern counties of Britain. Experiments have shown that some plants will prosper with warmer weather, such as fat-hen and stinging nettle which have maximum growth at 24–6 °C, but the grasses upright brome, *Bromus erectus*, and heath false brome, *Erectus pinnatum*, only have their maximum growth at 20–21 °C. Competition will see to it that the strongest survive and prosper, and in this case it will be fat-hen and stinging nettles.

The loss of the English bluebell wood might be hard to bear, but the loss of the natural stands of the now very rare native wild daffodil from English woods – an equally likely prospect with their preference for damp conditions – might just be too much.

The snake's-head fritillary, *Fritillaria meleagris*, has a nodding head, which is speckled in a variety of colours from pale pink to dark purple and white. Here they are growing in an 800-year-old alluvial meadow on the banks of the river Thames in Wiltshire at Cricklade

A roadside meadow dominated by bellflowers, *Campanula* sp., in southern France in May

The massed ranks of weld, *Reseda luteola*, grow alongside feverfew, *Tanacetum parthenium*, for seed production at Emorsgate Seeds, Norfolk

When not growing *en masse* in woods, bluebells, *Hyacinthoides non-scriptus*, often grow along English waysides in the company of stitchworts, *Stellaria* sp., and red campion, *Silene dioica*

May: ragged-robin, *Lychnis flos-cuculi*, and buttercups adorn this chalky meadow near Compton Down, a particularly fine nature reserve overlooking The Needles on the Isle of Wight, off the south coast of England

Morning glory, *Ipomoea purpurea*, uses the sturdy stems of the Mediterranean fennel, *Foeniculum vulgare*, to climb upwards and so decorate this small parcel of wild meadow in the Azores in mid-Atlantic in July

Red campion, *Silene dioica*, Queen Anne's lace or cow parsley, *Anthriscus sylvestris*, and docks sprawl together in this roadside meadow at Compton on the Isle of Wight in June. Red campion is very rarely bright red!

Corncockles and corn poppies make attractive partners in medieval meadow mixtures, as here, but they are familiar companions in the fields tilled by man too

In this floristic meadow in Battle, Sussex – an historic SSSI meadow – the pink inflorescences of common spotted-orchids, *Dactylorhiza fuchsii*, compete with burnets and ox-eye daisies, *Leucanthemum vulgare*. Later the meadow is overrun with yellow rattle, *Rhinanthus minor*

Cowslips not only thrive in these damp meadows next to streams, where they have great presence, but on very chalky soils where they are often diminutive. Here they are in the Cévennes, France in April

Many parts of England have this typical meadow scene with cuckooflower, or lady's-smock, *Cardamine pratensis*, conferring a pastel shade to the green meadow – but this is Bavaria, Germany in May, and is also a very typical scene throughout much of western Europe

Like an old grass aerodrome in full flower with dandelions, North Meadow at Cricklade, Wiltshire harbours the largest natural population of snake's-head fritillaries, *Fritillaria meleagris*, in Britain. The dandelions, *Taraxacum officinalis*, take over when the fritillaries start to wane

Tufted vetch, *Vicia cracca*, has the ability in the warmer Mediterranean climate of making a colourful meadow out of itself, creeping over the field as it laps up the heat. In Britain its growth is much more modest and it is more likely to be seen climbing up hedgerows. Here it is seen in Hérault, France in May

Salvias, poppies and arabis share the poor soils of this calcareous area of France – in Hérault – which make a lively meadow in June

Cuckooflower, *Cardamine pratensis*, in a woodland glade can create a natural monoculture, attracting the attention of the orange-tip, *Anthocharis cardamines*, which breeds there

An alternative for a lawn is this wild grassy area sown from a blended meadow mix, comprising crested dog's-tail, *Cynosurus cristatus*, meadow barley, *Hordeum secalinum*, and quaking-grass, *Briza media*

Old-fashioned hay meadows like this one in East Sussex can be created in a year from wildflower seed sown on a prepared site. Ox-eye daisy, *Leucanthemum vulgare*, is always successful since it comes up *en masse* in its first year and obscures other species which grow up in later years. The meadow here is at Wheel Park Farm, Westfield, East Sussex

Plume knapweed, *Centaurea nervosa*, and yarrow, *Achillea millefolium*, dominate this Alpine meadow at about 1,000 metres on the Massif of Aigoual in Hérault, southern France

A wild seed mixture is successfully established in these North American woods

Woodland glades in North America, in general terms, have a slightly different look to European ones. On much of the eastern coast of North America there are swamp cypress woodlands, which seem to go on endlessly – where they have not been exploited by man. In these watery woodland habitats, in the south, there are no glades, just expanses of water or floating islands – like mini-meadows, such as those found in the Okefenokee swamp (Georgia) where groups of handsome sandhill cranes graze, and cattle egrets and large herons find food. It is on these floating meadows that alligators also haul themselves out to bask in the sun, always keeping a beady eye out for danger, or for food such as a bird or deer to lunge at and drag underwater and drown – all in a space of five seconds.

On drier ground where hickory, live oaks and native magnolias occur, there would always have been glades. Here, master trees were felled by hurricanes, or the effects of fungi or, latterly, by North American Indians. It is in such places that the noise of woodpeckers and sapsuckers would have been heard working hard at old timbers – their brains naturally cushioned against harmful cerebral vibrations – hammering the wood with their tough bills. North America is very rich in woodpeckers, many bright red with black and white markings.

Glades in these woods today still harbour the magnificent native turkey, or 'gobbler' as it is known in the south, a fine bird which appears much larger than modern varieties. One can get a feeling of how common these gobblers once were since they are now still relatively common in some preserved woodlands (for example, along the Natchez Trace, Mississippi, an ancient trail), where one can suddenly disturb a group of them in a woodland glade, or in other 'improved' areas and see a group of them break out of the woodland on to a golf course! Early explorers seem always to have mentioned their abundance on their travels, and turkey-hunting remains an enthusiastic pastime. Turkeys used to be so common that boys would throw stones at them for fun. The brilliant illustrator John James Audubon (1785–1851) made famous the wild turkey of the glades, complete with its entourage of chicks running through the grass.

It would have been a delight to be one of those first explorers of the woods and glades of America. The glades would have been bright with wild flowers, native vines and climbers, gay with butterflies and other insects, full with huge flocks of robins (the American variety – as opposed to the different European robin) stripping the winter harvest of wild berries, and there would always have been the opportunity of coming face to face with a native grizzly bear or sneaking a view of the native American puma, now sadly much reduced in population.

Notes

1. Rackham, O., 1988, pp. 3–6, and 1992, personal communication.
2. The bluebell in England is different from the plant known as the bluebell in Scotland, for the English *Hyacinthoides non-scriptus* is known as the harebell or campanula in Scotland.
3. The press always seem to have a field-day when they report on likely looking pieces of interesting scientific information such as indicator species – but often only 1 per cent of the story is told. There are at least a hundred indicator species of woodlands, including wild flowers, ferns and lichens and it is a competent botanist who can walk nonchalantly through a wood and declare its age. Dog's mercury has been picked on as a typical indicator species, and has been written about in *The Times* among others. It was also the subject of controversy earlier this century, as it still is, regarding its real habitat. Does it grow on the flat in beech woods, or on the slopes where the drainage is better. Check this out yourself and look for the exceptions.
4. Peterken, G., 1981, p. 234.

CHAPTER 8
ALPINE MEADOWS

These fortunate people who have walked over the high Alpine
pastures of Switzerland or French Savoy or the Austrian Dolomites
will know what I mean. In that clean, pure air, fresh as iced water
and fruity as a glass of hock, the bright flowers bejewel the turf and
cluster up against the natural outcrops of grey rock, edging the quick,
narrow rills, silvery as minnows as they trickle from their sources:
blowing in the mountain breeze and crouching inch-low to the ground
in an instinct of self-protection against the mountain gales.

Vita Sackville-West, *Garden Book*, 1968, pp. 64–5.

Some people think that Alpine meadows are the sweetest of all meadow types – they may be the most dazzling, the most startling and the most arresting, but they are also a distinct group with highly characteristic attributes. Lowland meadows can be just as exciting in their own way. It is the flowers which give these different sorts of meadows their individual flavours.

The word 'Alpine' presupposes a European connection with its association with the Alps of southern Europe, which embrace parts of northern Italy, eastern France, southern Germany, Switzerland and Austria. The definition of what is, and what is not, Alpine is proposed by botanists who study Alpine flowers as anything above 1,000 metres in altitude.[1] Many lowland plants – for example, dandelion, dog's mercury, silver birch, wood oxalis, wortleberry – occur above this and may therefore be included as living in Alpine areas, but the true Alpine species are those that are not found in lowlands. Most true Alpine species stay above 1,500 metres, and are indeed found much higher.

Three separate Alpine areas are recognized. First, there is the sub-Alpine zone, which is the area up to the tree-line. The height varies; for instance, it is about 1,000 metres in Scotland, 2,000 metres in the Swiss Alps and about 3,700 metres in the west Himalayas. This zone may be occupied with colourful meadows and stunted trees and shrubs, especially at the limits of the tree growth line. The natural tree-line has been artificially lowered in a number of Alpine villages as the need for pastures increased in the past. The tree-line for coniferous trees – pines, junipers, etc. – is generally higher than that for deciduous trees such as beech and oak.

The second zone, the true Alpine plant zone occurs above the tree-line to about 3,500 metres where the soil becomes a little more poor, the meadows have shorter vegetation and the plants themselves may have large colourful flowers compared with their relatively small leaves.

It is in the high Alpine plant zone, however, that the most interesting plants occur which give Alpine meadows their claim to botanical fame. There is a limit to all plant growth in the mountains, and this is at about 4,000 metres. The highest point for high Alpine pastures is about 3,000 metres and that for hay meadows is about 2,000 metres.

Alpine flowers and Alpine meadows can be found elsewhere in the world in these zones, whether in the Sierra Nevada in North America or in the Snowy Mountains of Australia, the equatorial mountains of Africa, the Himalayas in Nepal, the Andes of South America, in Greenland or in New Zealand.[2]

Table 8.1 Typical Alpine flowers

Alpine meadows may be resplendent with dandelion, ragged-robin, yellow buttercup, milk parsley and red campion, all of which are also found in the lowlands. The following meadow species are restricted principally to Alpine areas. An indication is given as to whether they contribute to creating the overall colour of a meadow (i.e. a 'meadow-maker' indicated as 'M'); whether they grow as patches in the wild ('P'), or are fairly well dispersed ('D'). Those found only in North America are marked 'NA', and those with a distribution which spans Europe, Asia and North America, some of them being circumpolar, are marked with an asterisk.

The sub-Alpine buttercup has the largest flowers of any North American buttercup; several varieties of the fringed gentian exist, including one, the Rocky Mountain variety, *thermalis*, which has been adopted as the Yellowstone National Park flower. Parry's primrose is found in wetter places, but is accompanied by a carrion smell which presumably attracts the humming-birds which feed on the nectar from its pink flowers.

Common name	Scientific name	NA	M	P	D
Alpine butterwort	*Pinguicula alpina*				D
Alpine columbine	*Aquilegia alpina*			P	
Alpine forget-me-not	*Myosotis alpina*			P	
*Alpine forget-me-not	*Eritrichium nanum*				
Alpine snowbell	*Soldanella alpina*			P	
Alpine spring beauty	*Claytonia lanceolata*	NA			
Alpine trefoil, bird's-foot	*Lotus alpinus*			P	
Alpinrose	*Rhododendron ferrugineum*		M	P	
Auricula	*Primula auricula*				D
*Bistort, viviparous	*Polygonum viviparum*				
Buttercup, aconite-leaved	*Ranunculus aconitifolia*		M		
Buttercup, snow	*Ranunculus eschscholtzii*	NA			
*Campion, moss	*Silene acaulis*				
Garland flower	*Daphne cneorum*			P	
*Gentian, fringed	*Gentianopsis detonsa*				
Gentian, great yellow	*Gentiana lutea*				D
Gentian, spring	*Gentiana verna*			P	
Gentian, trumpet	*Gentiana acaulis*			P	
Globeflower	*Troillus europeae*		M		
Monk's-hood	*Aconitum napellus*				D
*Old man of the Mountain	*Hymenoxys grandiflora*	NA			
Oxlip	*Primula elatior*		M		
Primrose, bird's-eye	*Primula farinosa*		M		
Primrose, Parry's	*Primula parryi*	NA			
*Sneezeweed, Yarrow, Milfoil	*Achillea millefolium*				
Yellow rattle, greater	*Rhinanthus alectorolophus*		M		

In woods, or by them

Common name	Scientific name	NA	M	P	D
Alpine clematis	*Clematis alpina*				
Bilberry	*Vaccinium myrtillus*				
Butterfly, orchid, greater	*Platanthera chlorantha*				
Ground-elder	*Aegopodium podagraria*		M		
Hepatica	*Hepatica nobilis*				
Lily-of-the-valley	*Convallaria majalis*				
Lily, martagon	*Lilium martagon*				
Mercury, dog's	*Mercuralis perennis*			P	
Solomon's-seal	*Polygonatum multiflorum*				
Violet, yellow wood	*Viola biflora*				

Alpine meadows have always been acclaimed as good grazing grounds for cattle, and many tourists and walkers will have heard the jangling of cowbells typical of these Alpine slopes. So the meadows are really pastures; in fact, the two, 'meadows' and 'pastures' go hand in hand, for the meadows are mostly by courtesy of man's grazing regimes. Having to

Lady's mantle

make meadows and pastures distinct from one another is a trifle unrealistic since they have rather nebulous definitions, and in fact Tosco recognizes 'pasture-meadows', which he defines as 'meadows that can be harvested and grazed'.

Scything of the lush vegetation at lower levels on the valley bottoms has also contributed to meadows' survival. The short turf at higher levels is the effect of altitude and exposure on the plants, which tend to grow in a very stunted and miniaturized manner. The soil which supports the Alpine flora is technically called 'Alpine Meadow Soil', a classification unique to this situation, and it is characterized by being found above the tree-line, and by being shallow and stony with a thin layer of leaf litter and duff (a fibrous material of leaf decomposition). It is usually strongly acidic, which means that plants like Alpine heaths and rhododendrons can survive.

The diverse range of plants in Alpine meadows was always thought of as being ideal for cows, for their milk was rich, creamy and plentiful. In fact, at the end of the last century Ludwig Schröter[3] quoted an old herdsman's saying which summed up the four most beneficial plants as 'the best alpine fodder-plants':

> *Romeye, Muttern und Adelgras,*
> *Das Bese ist, was Chueli frass.*

These plants can be identified today as, in order: baldmoney or spignel, *Meum athamanticum*, an aromatic member of the carrot family; Alpine plantain, *Plantago alpina*; mountain plantain – a form of the previous species; and, finally, viviparous Alpine meadow-grass, *Poa alpina*. Spignel was particularly attractive to cattle who especially sought it out, and it was a good 'green fodder crop highly esteemed from earliest times'. Interestingly, the Alpine plantain was recognized by its odour, which was very similar to a Swiss cheese called Schabzieger.

In Alpine areas the seasonal movement of animals, usually sheep, from one area of pasture to another, and back again took place. The usual form of transhumance was from the valleys in the spring to new pastures on the mountain-tops which blossom with fresh green grass immediately the snows melt. In France, for example, where the tradition of transhumance is thousands of years old, there are special droveways – *drailes* – along which the sheep were driven, and in later centuries these droveways took precedence over new highways cut through mountain areas. One such road in the more rugged part of the Cévennes mountains in the *département* of Gard passes underneath a bridge which was built especially for the sheep. The sheep would go up to the mountain pastures in the spring and return in late summer. The journey in each direction would take a few days, and the three to four thousand sheep would be accompanied by a few shepherds and their dogs. The procession of sheep through the villages on their return would take a day or two. Today, the driving of the sheep is disappearing rapidly, and is being replaced by juggernauts which take the animals to and fro in just a few hours.

Feeding on the higher pastures certainly put plenty of flesh on to the sheep, and flavoured their flesh with aromatic herbs. In the past the flavour of the mutton was directly proportional to the manner of seasons the animal had been moved from one pasture to another, each of which built up its network of sinews on ever-tough muscles.

These are the animals which have done so much to maintain the mountain meadows of Europe (the animals decorated with black pom-poms are male) – their annual transhumance to Alpine meadows helps to rid the meadows of invasive scrub. At the turn of the century many of Europe's mountain-tops were grassy meadows, but now increasing afforestation and a drastic decline in transhumance has changed the look of the mountains

France, Italy and Germany have a tradition of transhumance stretching back thousands of years, moving their livestock to higher mountain-top pastures immediately the snows melted, and in Germany their white cows were, and are still, taken up to high pastures. In the west of Ireland, the movement of animals is completely different. The modest mountains of the Burren in County Clare are actually warmer in winter than the valleys, so a reverse transhumance has always occurred there. Some of the valleys

Cows, sheep and goats descend the precipitous Bavarian Alpine paths to the lowland valleys at the end of the summer. The noise of the cows' bells would ring out over the hills and wake everyone in the villages through which they passed. Accompanying them on this transhumance are two shepherds, one of whom is holding a lamb born on the Alpine pastures

actually fill up with 'disappearing' turlochs – lakes which appear after rain and in winter and then are swallowed up into subterranean caves in this limestone area – so that pasturing bullocks in the valleys in winter is dangerous. The Irish in these parts take their animals to the mountains for the winter and the fertile valleys in the summer. The west coast of Ireland is fortunate since it is warmed by the North Atlantic drift and many parts are frost-free all year, allowing meadow grasses to grow throughout the year, something that is not found anywhere else in north-western Europe. The extra growing period over the winter is invaluable for raising animals.

Traditional transhumance was also introduced to the western part of North America during the last century when sheep were regularly walked from the fertile San Francisco valley – which currently plays host to citrus and vine crops – up to the alpine pastures exposed high up in the High Sierras, part of the Rocky Mountains.

The rich green colour of the Bavarian meadows is very much a result of the high rainfall, and the farmers, clad in *lederhosen*, braces and hats, take several crops of grass off each year, laying the long green grass and flowers on racks to dry in the sun and wind.

Nature's wild garden has taken rather a shock in the last few decades; the abundance of wild flowers is not what it used to be. Some Alpine flowers are now found only in places where man and beast have found it difficult or impossible to get to 'to improve'. Some flowers are now better represented along roadside verges, or around fields or in squelchy bogs, or on inaccessible cliff ledges, or on really rocky terrain where the last Ice Age deposited horrendous piles of morainic materials including jagged rocks and debris. In Bavaria where farmers used to have ten cows they now have thirty, and this is a source of some disquiet since the meat goes mostly to Italian tables.

The Alpine meadows are certainly very green but many have lost their wonderful floral diversity. Several flowers still offer a showing, despite surviving in incredibly short turf with constant cropping by man and beast. Gentians, surprisingly, do very well in this man-managed habitat and the tall yellow gentians stand proud in Alpine meadows defying the cows with their nasty-tasting leaves. The early gentians *Gentiana verna* and *Gentiana acaulis* have mostly flowered and fruited before the animals are moved to these high Alpine valleys for summer feeding. In the lusher areas

The common star-of-Bethlehem, *Ornithogalum umbellatum*, grows in Alpine meadows alongside bluish festucas, and is completely ignored by sheep, which sense that it is poisonous

and on banks the large willow-leaved gentian grows so enthusiastically in the autumn it overflows with ladders of blue flowers on its long stems.

At different times of the year Alpine meadows sport different colours. In the valleys they may be aglow with dandelions in the spring, higher-up pink with red campion or yellow with oxlips or thinly-spread auriculas, and in the autumn pink with a suffusion of naked ladies, or colchicum. Colchicums are abundant on some roadside verges and make a stunning visual impact on those touring. How coveted are these in England, where closely-packed groups are grown in orchard turf, as for instance at Sissinghurst, in a very atypical way to that in which they grow in the wild.

During the summer the meadows are also punctuated with the blue of monk's-hood – a regular plant in the English herbaceous border. This European plant was supposedly introduced to Britain by surreptitious monks keen to have a poison which could easily be slipped into a goblet of wine. The survival of many meadow plants is by virtue of their relative toxicity to grazing animals, such as ibex, chamois, mouflon, rabbits, sheep and cattle in the Alps. White and yellow buttercups, blue monk's-hood, and the great yellow gentian are all *habitués* of Alpine meadows because their leaves are packed with poisons. The poisons are manufactured by the plants from raw materials as a defence, but the plants themselves are not harmed by them.[4]

Red clover is common, especially around the edges of meadows, and consequently attracts many butterflies, such as clouded yellows, tiny blues and whites. The gradual loss of Alpine meadows has reduced the frequency of the two big swallowtail butterflies, the ordinary yellow and black one and the 'scarce swallowtail' with its long tails. In this age of greater agricultural productivity – at least in Bavaria where it is continuing to increase, although it is reducing elsewhere in Europe – it is regrettable that many an Alpine meadow has been lost to maize, which is so undistinguished wherever it occurs in the world.

One of the great joys of studying Alpine flowers is in watching the emergence of flowers such as the pale yellow auriculas through the snow as it melts around them. The contrast between the brilliance of the flower's colour and the white snow is almost unbelievable. The sheer bravado and cheekiness of flowers pushing their way in an unforgiving manner through the old leaves of the last season and the snow is quite remarkable. And to be covered each day with snowfall, only to reappear the following day with renewed vigour is astounding. William Robinson, in the nineteenth century, described his experience while plant-hunting in the Italian Alps:

> Soon we reached the meadow land towards the bottom of the warm valley, and found this Piedmontese meadow almost blue with forget-me-nots and strange harebells, enlivened by orchids, and jewelled here and there with St. Bruno's lily (*Paradisia liliastrum*).[5]

Monk's-hood, *Aconitum napellus*, is a typical Alpine species, though much grown in gardens as an herbaceous perennial. It is poisonous and is thought to have been introduced to Britain by monks for surreptitious use in goblets of wine

So much for plants. They are the important indicators of Alpine meadows and pastures because they are so numerous. There are, though, several insect species and, to a lesser extent, mammals that are also indicators of Alpine areas, but they are of course dependent upon the plants for their survival. It is the classic chicken-or-egg situation. Which came first, the insects or the plants, for each is dependent upon the other for survival? The plants need the insects for pollination and the insects need plants for their larval and adult foodplants. There is no other reason for Alpine flowers to be so bright and colourful (to us) than because they have to attract insects – even though insects will see the flowers differently, using wavelengths of light unavailable to us. In fact, some Alpine species seem to have their own specially bright colours, but this is very much a product of how we happen to perceive them in the clear light which is rich in ultra-violet, and the colours have not really evolved at all.

In the high Arctic the grasslands and tundra support strong populations of a few species of buttlerflies which can cope well with the particular climate. Butterflies swarm over Alpine and sub-Alpine meadows in the tundra. In North America species like the small mormon fritillary can be exceedingly plentiful visiting asters and wild corn lilies, and they help to make up the great profusion of wildlife which takes advantage of the short but sunny summer weather.

Mountain fritillaries and silver meadow fritillaries (otherwise known in Europe as the pearl-bordered fritillary) are other members of the successful fritillary group of butterflies which frequent these latitudes. The weather is not always clement in the Arctic, and some meadow butterflies have adopted interesting ways of coping. The bog fritillary crawls into mosses and heaths and other low vegetation to see out the bad weather, and the dingy Arctic fritillary butterfly is more often seen walking around the habitat than trying to fly around it. Other adaptations that butterflies have made is to cram much of their courtship into the limited periods that the sun peeks out from behind rapidly passing clouds.

Aggregating in small groups, and often in warm hollows, the butterflies are best placed to become active as soon as the sun bursts from behind a cloud, and to get in as much courtship as possible, perhaps a unit of copulation, before the sun disappears again, which it is apt to do. The butterflies must also avoid sudden decreases in temperature caused by passing snow flurries and this they have done by having blood reinforced

The apollo butterflies, *Parnassia* sp., frequent the tops of mountains in Europe and North America and breed on stonecrops, *Sedum* sp. Both food plant and butterfly are vulnerable to change in their environment

with the addition of either glycerol or the carbohydrate sorbitol. Apollos have both a greasy look and feel, and this is due to glycerol, the insect's natural anti-freeze.

Table 8.2 Meadow butterflies of the Arctic

*Dingy Arctic fritillary	*Boloria frigga*
Mormon fritillary	*Speyeria mormonia*
*Mountain fritillary	*Boloria napaea*
*Polar fritillary	*Boloria polaris*
*Purple bog fritillary	*Boloria titania*
*Silver meadow fritillary	*Boloria selene*
*Willow-bog fritillary	*Boloria frigga*

★ found in the Arctic of both the New and Old Worlds.

Among the butterflies, the apollos and *Erebias*, or Alpine ringlets, are those groups which are indicators of Alpine areas and occur up to great altitudes. In complete contrast to each other, the apollos are whitish with black spots, the *Erebias* are deep brown, almost black, with reddish markings. The darkness of the spotting helps these insects to absorb the sunshine which warms their muscles for flight. It is the smallest of the apollos which is found both in North America and in Europe, while its bigger relative is only found in the mountains of Europe. It is, now though, severely threatened, principally because of habitat destruction – often skiing developments. On the other hand, the *Erebias* are almost super-numerous in the mountains of Europe – there are over twenty species and the distribution of some of these includes the Far East – yet only one species, the Arctic ringlet, *Erebia disa*, is also found in North America. The reason for this disparity is that many of the North American species were originally colonized by the very slow movement of organisms from the Old World to the New over the land bridge now occupied by the Bering Strait and the Aleutian Islands.

There are often many snails and slugs in Alpine meadows since these invertebrates thrive in damp conditions. The largest of the snails in European Alpine meadows is the Roman snail which is in many cases much larger and heavier than a golf ball. Those Roman snails found in southern English meadows, now so infrequently, are never that corpulent. They are descendants of those snails introduced by the Romans two thousand years ago. Beetles too rove around the meadows and some of them specialize in eating the smaller snail species, especially the larvae and adults of glow-worms. Wood ants are typically found in Alpine meadows, their huge brown nests often at the edge of the forest, or occasionally in the open not far from the trees, some taller than man. During the winter the nests are covered in snow, which acts as an insulation for the ants' survival to the next spring.

Insectivorous birds do well over Bavarian meadows since the slurry from cows is perpetually spread on the fields (to the detriment of Alpine streams and their nitrogen-sensitive wildlife). Wagtails and migratory black redstarts and swallows have a prosperous time with their families.

Up to a hundred years ago Alpine villages in Europe and their attractive meadows were visited by aristocrats and high-ranking military officers and their families, sometimes on a grand tour of Europe. Horticulturalists and garden enthusiasts visited as well, but the mass of tourists that we know of today were then unknown. This brought about an enthusiasm for Alpine gardening which was further encouraged by exercises in Alpine gardening by the father of wild flower gardening William Robinson and by Vita Sackville-West.

Typical Alpine meadows and pastures in Bavaria

Part of the enthusiasm for meadows today is in the creation of meadows at home; but it is not a new idea, as illustrated here in William Robinson's book from the last century. One of his enthusiasms was Alpine meadows, growing marginal Alpines with a border of hardy flowers

William Robinson had visited the Alpine meadows and pastures in France and Italy in the 1880s and had been very impressed. He had also travelled across the American Sierras and seen the Alpine plants there, always putting them in a gardening context:

> There is as much difference in size between our common border phloxes – the parents of which are wild in the middle and southern states of America – and the diminutive mountain phloxes I speak of, as between swans and humming-birds. The alpine phloxes of the Rocky Mountains or the Sierra are as indispensible to the choice-collector of alpine plants as the Gentians or the Primulas. Very few of them have been introduced. . . . everywhere on bare places there are tufts of dwarf, bush-like penstemons. . . . the orange lily creeps up high on the rocks of Piedmont; here Washington's Lily – a tall, noble and fragrant kind.[6]

Gravetye Manor, Sussex, the home of William Robinson (1838–1935), the father of the English flower garden, who liked wild Alpine meadows

At home on his estate at Gravetye Manor, near East Grinstead, William Robinson made his own Alpine meadow from a south-facing slope of ground which ran down from the house towards a stream. He believed that Alpine species which do well in Alpine conditions should do well in Britain since our relatively cool and damp climate is similar to that found in the mountains. He was most impressed with the Piedmont meadows in the Italian Alps which 'were blue with forget-me-nots and strange harebells, enlivened by orchids and jewelled here and there with St Bruno's lilies whose flowers were nearly two inches long',[7] and walked over many passes searching for rare ranunculi, scarce silenes and superb saxifrages. Back in Sussex he leased out a part of his estate to Wil Ingwersen for his Alpine nursery, who later became a leading Alpine nurseryman. Robinson later wrote *Alpine Flowers for English Gardens.*

Vita Sackville-West encouraged the planting of Alpine lawns of thyme similar to the prostrate assemblage of plants found in the Alps, and recommended 'little mints' – yellow stonecrop, camomile, blue speedwell, the trumpet gentian (if you were able to grow it), *Raoulia australis*, wild violets and *Saxifraga oppositifolia.*

This enthusiasm for Alpine gardens extended to the whole contemporary court of Robinson and Gertrude Jeykll, as well as their friend Miss Willmott. Miss Willmott had been left £140,000 by her father and a grand estate, Warley Place in Essex, where she developed her considerable gardening skills.[8] Warley had once, apparently, been owned by John Evelyn[9] and he had planted not only the sweet chestnut trees at Warley but the early English crocus, *Crocus vernus*, in the meadows there, to complement the daffodil bank and the pleasure gardens. These meadows had originally been part of the English countryside and retained quaint meadow names such as the Hoppit, the Doll's Meadow, and the Well Mead.

The key to Miss Willmott's successful creation of Alpine meadows was the employment at Warley of a young Swiss apprentice Jacob Maurer, in 1894, who no doubt brought with him a natural understanding of the way plants grew in the Alps. Here on an Essex hillside blossomed *Primula sikkimensis, Primula sinensis, Dianthus gracilis, Dianthus plumarius, Campanula pusilla, Gentiana verna, Gentiana acaulis, Sempervirens, Aethinena, Daphne odora* and many others. *Trillium, Cistus* and *Erodium* diverted the eye, the murmur of the stream and the movement of countless butterflies making the Alpine garden an entrancing and hypnotic place to wander in. Just like Robinson's alpine garden at Gravetye Manor, Warley Place's wild garden was full of introduced plants from around the world. There were other English wilder areas one assumes, since Audrey Le Lièvre writes of her:

> There was a glimpse to be had from this lane of the Well Mead garden, with its roses, grapes, figs and vegetables, and of the wild garden, where all the wild flowers of Essex flourished and hybridised with

wild flowers from all the continent of Europe, planted amidst the English grasses and left to accumulate themselves.[10]

Perhaps one of the most admired Alpine gardens is at Wisley, the Surrey grounds belonging to the Royal Horticultural Society of London. On a gentle slope leading down to a very small rivulet swathes of tiny narcissi crowd out masses of spring crocuses in the verdant green grass.

Alpine gardening is not, though, everyone's passion, as is evident from the scathing comments of Russell Page, the noted garden designer in Europe, writing in 1962:

In the British Isles, at least, one form of miniature garden is endemic. That is the artificially introduced rock or alpine garden in all its forms, whether a bank set with chunks of broken concrete, or the faithful reproduction of a few yards of alpine scree or moraine, or an elaborate composition of carefully bedded rocks with mountain cascades and discreet and reticent planting. I too have worshipped for many years at such shrines; but the enjoyment of this kind of gardening is an act of faith. Here you must deliberately subtract yourself from the surroundings, change the focus of your vision, and enter into the small and exquisite world of alpine plants where pebbles and grains of sand have a crystalline intensity, where the flowers of gentian and eritrichium seem to contain both lakes and sky, and where two large stones and a trickle of water are as mysterious as a Himalayan gorge. But this is a game of make-believe and, try as you may by design or by planting to lead down to the reduced scale of such a garden, it remains an anomaly and thus an enemy of style.[11]

As for conservation, there was a time, almost in living memory, when conservation was not really understood, when it was the done thing to collect wild flowers. For instance, Schröter assumes that his readers will collect the flowers of Alpine soldanella and place them in a book as soon as possible since the petals are so fragile. And it was typical of William Robinson that he searched all day in the Alps for a particular plant, only to dig up the only plant he found. The natural world is now recognized as a much more fragile place, and, fortunately, more respect is given to its fascinating flora and fauna.

Certain meadow species have been collected to the point of extinction in places, including the lady's-slipper orchid, *Cypripedium calceolus*, and the edelweiss, *Leontopodium alpinum*. These are more often found in gardens and cemeteries than in Alpine meadows now

Unfortunately Alpine flowers are still picked by more than a minority of people. Picked flowers, cast down as limp rejects, are still found along the Alpine paths today. Walkers and naturalists in the Alps will now perhaps never see the edelweiss or the lady's-slipper orchid, unless in a private garden or, more often than not, in a cemetery, for these prizes of the Alps have been picked to the point of extinction over the years.

There have been efforts to conserve Alpine meadows from the effects of skiing, walking and agriculture.[12, 13] Some of these have centred on one of the highest of Alpine villages in western Europe, Obergurgl (1,930 metres) in the Austrian Tyrol, which has experienced problems typical of many Alpine villages.

The productivity of the Alpine meadows of Obergurgl controlled the population for centuries, ever since the community was founded in 1400. Only about 120 people could live in this tiny village as a self-sufficient unit based on the meadows, since there was no contact with the outside world. In 1830 marriages were banned to hold down the population to that which could effectively survive on the products of the meadows, and in 1850 121 villagers had to emigrate to keep the population stable. Men married late, on average at about forty-three years of age, with women marrying at thirty-six, in order to limit population growth. More meadows were reclaimed by reducing the tree-line by 400 metres.

One of the active measures to conserve meadows in recent decades has been to enclose various portions of the meadows away from grazers and man, so that regeneration of the flora is encouraged. This has only been in effect for ten years, through the offices of the United Nations Educational, Scientific and Cultural Organisation,[14] and so far few results are available.

The opening-up of Obergurgl to tourism started about 110 years ago, and there has now been a progressive shift away from agriculture based on the Alpine meadows to tourism which is now far more profitable. The flat valley bottom meadows have been quickly swallowed up for the development of hotels and other tourist attractions, and the steep mountain meadows are degraded as ski-runs.

A recent report on the state of the Alps produced by a Member of the European Parliament makes sober reading.[15] Skiing and all its peripheral activities, such as the necessary infrastructure and hotels, have had a major impact on the region. Official statistics estimate that there are now about 3,000 cable railways and 13,000 ski-lifts. Between them there are about

Cows have also been blamed for the demise of many mountain wild flowers and butterflies. Here in Bavaria and in the Tyrol the meadows never looked so green, with a lack of Alpine species

The widespread use of mountain-tops for skiing, as here in the Alps, has eliminated many of the last sanctuaries of Alpine species, for which these mountain-tops were their refuges. Such is especially the case with the apollo butterflies. In Colorado, USA, where there is much skiing development, there are over a thousand mountains which are more than 1.5 kilometres high, and the Alpine area is six times greater than that of Switzerland

1.3 million transports of people each year, enough to accommodate the world's population on the Alps in four years. About two-thirds of the Alps habitats are developed and affected by man, and the dreaded spread of tourism is a *Landschaftsfresser*, or 'landscape-eater'. There are moves to protect what is left. There are also plans to compensate farmers for land not farmed, as has been tried successfully in Britain. There are also *Skilauf-grosen*, or solidarity contributions, from the skiers to help conserve the Alpine landscape, and protected areas, *Ruhezonen*, which should not be disturbed by man. Perhaps the Alpine meadows will find refuge in these new intiatives.

Notes

1. Grey-Wilson, C., 1979, p. 7.
2. Tosco, U., 1974.

3. Schröter, C., 1904. Schröter also cites another book, *The Alpine Fodderplants*, Berne, K.J. Wyss, 1889.
4. Interestingly, it is these plant poisons which are so readily used in pharmacology since it is well-known that small amounts of poisons can have efficacious effects on man. See, for instance, Dr Rainer Schunk's *Heilkraft aus Heilpflanzen* (Abtswind, Kaulfuss-Verlag Abtswind, 1990), which is about the healing properties of 150 species of plants, many of them Alpine.
5. Robinson, W., 1879, p. 124.
6. Robinson, W., 1870, p. 148, while visiting the Sierras by train and on foot. The Washington's lily, *Lilium washingtonianum*, is a native Californian plant whose variety *minus* is the Shasta lily.
7. Allan, Mea, 1973, p. 87. It is especially worth reading chapter 8, 'Gleanings from the Alps', which is a very light-hearted account of his journeys.
8. For a woman of Miss Willmott's stature and achievements it is a pity that her life has been somewhat shelved away to almost obscurity. She and Warley are remembered as, for instance, *Tulipa willmottiae*, *Iris 'Warlsind'* and *Iris warleyensis*. She encouraged Sir Thomas Hanbury to buy Wisley and give it to the Royal Horticultural Society (RHS), and she tried hard to get the management at the reluctant RHS to accept this gift. In her prime she ran three gardens (Warley Place; Villa d'Aimable in Tresserve, Switzerland; and Boccanegra, Ventimeglia, Italy and employed 104 gardeners. She provided plant material for Kew, and the Arnold Arboretum in the USA and part-financed Ernest Wilson's collecting trip to China. But the other side of the story is that she could not manage her financial affairs and spent all her legacy. Finally, she was hounded by various authorities, including the local council for not paying her rates. The RHS stepped in and paid them, a gesture beyond contemplation today.
9. John Evelyn is more well-known for his gardening on the south side of the Thames estuary in north-west Kent.
10. Le Lièvre, A., 1980.
11. Page, R., 1983, p. 59.
12. Sage, B., 1979, pp. 30–1.
13. Partsch, K. and Zaunberger, K., 1990/91, pp. 22, 36.
14. Ibid.
15. Ibid.

Appendix

Meadows and Pastures in England, Wales and Scotland

The following table has been extracted from *The Macmillan Guide to Britain's Nature Reserves* (1984). Note that the meadows and pastures do not always constitute the main part of the named site. The list is not exhaustive since there are so many 'grassland' sites. Most of the meadows listed in the guide have been included. Before visiting the sites check to ascertain where further information is available.

County and Site	Description
ENGLAND	
Bedfordshire and Huntingdonshire	
Upwood Meadows	old meadow remnant
Woodwalton Fen	fenland remnant
Wymington Meadow	old meadow grassland
Cambridgeshire	
Chippenham Fen	unimproved wet meadows
Fleam Dyke	grassed over earthworks
Gamlingay Meadow	small damp heathland
Ouse Washes	fen meadow grassland
Soham Meadow	wet meadows
Triplow Meadows	damp meadows
Wicken Fen	relic fenland
Derbyshire	
Derbyshire Dales	limestone grassland
Devon	
Brownsham	heathy grassland
Dunasford and Meadhaydown	mixed valley woodland

Dorset
    Isle of Purbeck   limestone grassland
    Tadnoll Meadow   damp meadowland
    Whitenothe Undercliff   chalk grassland

Durham, Cleveland and Tyne and Wear
    Blackhall   coastal limestone grassland

Essex
    Hitchcok's Meadows   lime-rich grassland
    Loshes Meadow   woodland and meadow

Gloucestershire
    Daneway Banks   limestone grassland
    Rodborough Common   limestone grassland
    Slimbridge Wildfowl Sanctuary   grazing meadows

Hampshire and the Isle of Wight
    Broughton Down   chalk grassland
    Catherinton Down   chalk grassland
    Martin Down   chalk grassland
    Old Winchester Hill   chalk grassland
    St Catherine's Hill   chalk grassland
    Stockbridge Common Down   ungrazed downland
    Tennyson Down and the Needles   coastal chalk downland
    Titchfield Haven   grazing meadows by river
    Upper Titchfield Haven   meadow
    Wellington Country Park   meadowland
    Winnall Moors   water meadows

Hereford and Worcester
    Boynes Coppice and Meadow   ancient meadow
    Drake Street Meadow   ancient meadow
    Duke of York Meadow   ancient meadow
    Eades Meadow and Fosters Green ancient meadow
      Meadow   brookside meadows
    Knowles Coppice   unimproved hay meadow
    Long Meadow   old meadow grassland
    Melrose Farm Meadows   grassland with daffodils
    Wessington Pasture

Hertfordshire
    Alpine Meadow   chalk grassland
    Blagrove Common   rich damp meadow
    Hunsdon Meads   old meadow grassland

Kent
 Denton Bank   chalk grassland
 Eastcourt Meadows Country Park   estuary grassland
 Kemsing Downs   chalk grassland
 Lydden Downs   chalk grassland
 Oare Meadow   wet meadow
 Queendown Warren   chalk grassland
 Wye and Crundale Downs   chalk downland

Lancashire and Greater Manchester
 Gait Burrows   wetland meadows

Leicestershire and Rutland
 Cribb's Meadow   unimproved meadowland
 Herbert's Meadow   unimproved grassland
 Ulverscroft   meadow and marsh
 Wymondham Rough   unimproved grassland

Lincolnshire and South Humberside
 Baston Fen   flood meadow
 Heath's Meadow   small grassland hayfields
 Little Scrubb's Meadow   old grassland
 Moor Farm   pasture
 Red Hill   chalk grassland
 Sotby Meadows   old meadows

Norfolk
 Ouse Washes   winter flooded fen meadows
 Ringstead Downs   chalk downland

Northamptonshire and the Soke of Peterborough
 Barnack Hills and Holes   limestone grassland
 Castor Hanglands   grassland
 Glapthorn Cow Pasture   scrub

Northumberland
 Little Harle   unimproved flood meadows
 Strother Pond   old pasture

Nottinghamshire
 Clarborough   lime-rich grassland
 Eakring Meadows   damp meadowland
 West Burton Meadow   unimproved grassland

Oxfordshire
 Ashton Rowant   chalk grassland

Coleshill Meadow	old grassland
Foxholes	riverside meadow
Otmoor Rifle Range	damp old meadow grassland
Warburg	chalk grassland

Shropshire
Llynclys Common	grassland

Staffordshire
Alliomore Green Common	unimproved pasture
Deep Hayes Country Park	meadows
Eccleshaw Castle Mere	meadows
Mottey Meadows	old meadow grassland

Suffolk
Fox Fritillary Meadow	fritillary meadow
Gromford Meadow	wet old meadows
Lady's Mantle Meadow	ancient meadowland
Martin's Meadow	ancient meadowland
Mickfield Meadow	old meadow
Pashford Poors Pen	grassland

Surrey
Box Hill Country Park	chalk downland
Hackhurst Down	chalk downland
Headley Heath	chalk grassland
Headley Warren	chalk grassland
Thundry Meadows	wet meadowland

Sussex
Amberley Wild Brooks	rich flood meadows
Castle Hill	fine chalk grassland
Cuckmere Haven	downland
Filsham	water meadows
Kingley Vale	chalk grassland
Levin Down	chalk grassland
Rye Harbour	meadows
Seven Sisters Country Park	downland
Waltham Brooks	flood meadows

Warwickshire and West Midlands
Burton Dassett Country Park	hilly grassland
Draycote Meadows	old meadow grassland
Harbury Spoil Bank	lime-rich grassland
Oxhouse Farm	lime-rich grassland

Wiltshire
Barbury Castle Country Park	chalk downland
Hen Down	chalk downland
Lavington Hill	chalk grassland
North Meadow	old meadow grassland
Pepperbox Hill	rough chalk grassland
Pewsey Downs	open chalk grassland
Prescombe Down	chalk grassland
Upper Waterhay	old meadow grassland
Wylye Down	chalk downland

Yorkshire and North Humberside
Farndale	valley daffodil fields
Hornsea Mere	fields
Kiplingcotes Chalk Pit	chalk grassland
Malham Tarn	limestone grassland
Stockmoor Common	damp grassland
Thorpe Marsh	pasture
Wheldrake Ings	flood meadows
Yorkshire Dales National Park	upland

WALES

Dyfed
Craig Fawr	limestone grassland
Gwenffrwd-Dinas	pasture
Llyn Eiddwen	upland grassland
Rhos Glyn-yr-Helyg	wet pasture
Rosemoor	rough pasture

Glamorgan
Lavernock Point	limestone grassland
Ogmore Down	limestone grassland
Redley Cliff	coastal grassland

Gwent
Henllys Bog	damp grassland
Magor	relic fen
Ysgyryd Fawr	grassland

Gwynedd
Cors Goch	rich fen, limestone grassland
Gogarth	limestone grassland
Great Orme Nature Trails	limestone grassland, sea cliffs

Powys
    Lake Vyrnwy   grassland
    Ogof Ffynon Ddu   grassland

SCOTLAND

    Auchalton Meadow   lime-rich grassland
    Aberlady Bay   grassland
    Balranald, North Uist   machair
    Brerachan Meadows   uncultivated meadow
    Carradale   coastal grassland
    Dowalton   wet meadow
    Duns Castle   grassland
    Eigg   lime-rich upland area
    Feoch Meadows   meadow on lime-rich rock
    Insh Marshes   wet pasture
    Keltneyburn   meadow
    Loch Druidibeg, South Uist machair
    Seaton Cliffs   coastal cliffs
    St Ann's Head   grassland

FURTHER INFORMATION

Wildflower seed merchants and endangered species preservation organizations

BRITAIN

Ashton Wold Wild Flowers,
Ashton Wold,
Nr Peterborough,
PE8 5LZ.
Tel: 0832 73575
Catalogue available. Various seed mixtures including 'Ashton Wold Hay Meadow Seeds', 'Sudborough Green Lodge Meadow (SSSI)', 'Burnt Close' (67 species), 'Polo Field' (34 species), 'Wood Walton Fen (SSSI)', 'Prince of Wales mixture', 'Farmer's Nightmare Mixture', as well as potted wild flower plants.

BTCV Trees and Wildflowers,
The Old Estate Yard,
Newton St Loe,
Bath,
Avon,
BA2 9BR.
Tel: 0225 874018
Fax: 0225 874222
A wide variety of native trees and shrubs to create tiered field margins next to meadows.

John Chambers Wild Flower Seeds,
15 Westleigh Road,
Barton Seagrave,
Kettering,
Northamptonshire,
NN15 5AJ.
Tel: 0933 652562
Fax: 0933 652576
Comprehensive catalogue. Many seed mixes available including 'Natural Meadow', 'Asham Meads', 'Burnt Close', 'Cricklade Meadow', 'Pixie Meads', 'Cornfield Wildflowers' and a special collection of 'Meadow' plant seeds including bird's-foot trefoil, cowslip, harebell, kidney vetch and lady's bedstraw. There are also 36 'conservation organisation' mixtures which cater for most natural history and conservation interests. And for ornithologists there is a 'Meadow in a Can' songbird meadow mixture containing 31 plant species.

Chiltern Seeds,
Bortree Stile,
Ulverston,
Cumbria,
LA12 7PB.
Tel: 0229 581137
Comprehensive seed catalogue listing wild flowers of the British Isles.

Emorsgate Seeds,
Terrington Court,
Terrington St Clement,
King's Lynn,
Norfolk,
PE34 4NT.
Tel and fax: 0553 829028
Comprehensive catalogue available: 'Wild Flowers and Grasses for Creating Naturalistic Landscapes'. Also mixtures for habitat creation, including wild flower meadow, pond edge mixture, wild flower wood, cornfield. Wild flower plants.

Mr Fothergill's Seeds Ltd,
Kentford,
Newmarket,
Suffolk,
CB8 7QB.
Mail order only, catalogue available. Unusual worldwide range of wild flower mixtures, such as 'Australian mixed annuals', 'Alaskan wild flowers', 'Californian brilliant wild flowers', 'North American wild flowers', 'Wildflowers of the Holy Land', as well as 'British Cornfield Mixture' and 'British Wildflower mixture'.

Landlife Wildflowers Ltd,
The Old Police Station,
Lark Lane,
Liverpool,
L17 8UU.
Tel: 051 728 7011
Catalogue available. Comprehensive range of educational materials, such as gardening booklets, wild flower prints and transparencies, wild flower pack. Seed mixtures of the 'Wildflower Plant Collections' include 'Ordinary Flower Meadow', 'Woodland Glade', 'Drought' and 'Pondside', each containing 10 plant species, and 'Cornfield Collection', 'Wildflower seed and native British plants and bulbs' and nine separate mixtures available for spring to summer meadows and for meadows on calcareous soils.

Suffolk Herbs Ltd,
Sawyers Farm,
Little Cornard,
Sudbury,
Suffolk,
CO10 0NY.
Tel: 0787 227247
Fax: 0787 227258
Comprehensive catalogue and separates. Wild flower and grass conservation mixtures include 'Old Haymeadow Mixture' (two sorts: for clay and loam, and chalk and limestone), 'Watermeadow Mixture', 'Old Woodland Mixture', 'Sandy Soil Mixture', 'Pond Edge Mixture',

'Hedgerow Mixture', 'Flowers from Field and Hedgerow', 'Old Cornfield Mixture', and 'Mixture for Birds'. Posters of poppy fields and bluebell woods also available.

NORTH AMERICA

At least fourteen American states now have local chapters of The Native Plant Society, but only four widely-spaced ones are given here.

Applewood Seed Company,
5380 Vivian Street,
Arvada,
CO 80002,
USA.

California Native Plant Society,
2380 Ellsworth Street,
Berkeley,
CA 94704,
USA.

Canadian Wildflower Society,
1848 Liverpool Road,
Suite 110,
Pickering,
Ontario,
L1V 6M3
Canada.
Dedicated to the study, conservation and cultivation of North America's wild flowers and other wild flora. Publishes *Wildflower* magazine, which provides information on wild flower gardening techniques and features native plants suitable for the garden. Lists sources across North America for seeds and nursery-grown native plants.

Clyde Robin Seed Co.,
PO Box 2366,
Castro Valley,

CA 94546,
USA.
Tel: 415 785 0425
Stock regional wild flower and meadow mixes, such as 'North-eastern',
'North-western', 'South-western', 'Checkerboard north' (and south),
'Roadside Mix', 'Meadow in a Can', 'Wildflower Patch', 'Border Patch',
'Country Carpet', 'Petite Botanique', 'Blue and Gold Mix' and 'Good
Morning Sunshine'.

Florida Native Plant Society,

1203 Orange Avenue,
Winter Park,
FL 32789,
USA.

Gardens of the Blue Ridge,

PO Box 10,
Pineola,
NC 28662,
USA.
Tel: 704 733 2417
Native wild flowers, but no meadow mixes.

Greenhedges,

650 Montee de Liesse,
Montreal,
Quebec,
H4T 1N8,
Canada.

New Mexico Native Plant Society,

Box 5917,
Santa Fe,
NM 87502,
USA.

Washington Native Plant Society,
Botany Department,
University of Washington,
Seattle,
WA 98195,
USA.

Meadow conservation

BRITAIN

The Countryside Commission,
John Dower House,
Crescent Place,
Cheltenham,
Gloucester,
GL50 3RA.
Tel: 0242 521381
Fax: 0242 584270
Originator of the three-year 'Countryside Stewardship' project in 1991 which was financed by the government with the intention of re-creating wetland habitats including meadows, among other types of habitat.

Countryside Council for Wales,
Plas Penrhos,
Bangor,
Gwynedd,
LL57 2LQ.
Tel: 0248 30444
Concerned with meadow conservation in Wales.

English Nature,
Interpretive services,
Northminster House,
Nr Peterborough,
PE1 1UA.
Tel: 0733 340345

Publishes a number of relevant books on wild flowers, habitats and conservation. Concerned only with the welfare of the English countryside.

The Game Conservancy,
Burgate Manor,
Fordingbridge,
Hampshire,
SP6 1EF.
Tel: 0425 652381
Fax: 0425 655848
Catalogue available. Distributes a free leaflet on 'Conservation Headlands'.

Joint Nature Conservation Committee,
Monkston House,
City Road,
Peterborough,
PE1 IJY.
Tel: 0733 62626
Fax: 0733 555948
The UK Joint Nature Conservation Committee is the statutory body constituted by the Environmental Act 1990 responsible for research and advice on nature conservation at both UK and international level. It is formed by English Nature, the Nature Conservancy for Scotland and the Countryside Council for Wales, together with independent members and representatives from Northern Ireland and from the Countryside Commission, and is supported by specialist staff.

Plantlife,
c/o The Natural History Museum,
Cromwell Road,
London,
SW7 5BD.
Tel: 071 938 9055
Concerned with the conservation of British native plants.

The Royal Society for Nature Conservation (RSNC), Wildlife Trusts Partnership

The Green,
Witham Park,
Waterside South,
Lincoln,
LN5 7JR.
Tel: 0522 544400
The parent body of the Wildlife Trusts Partnership (47 Wildlife Trusts, 212,000 members). Regularly raises awareness of wild flowers and is much concerned with meadows (see RSNC, 1991). Wildlife Trusts own or manage meadows, and these are open to the public.

The Royal Society for the Protection of Birds (RSPB),

The Lodge,
Sandy,
Bedfordshire,
SG19 2DL.
Tel: 0767 80551
Long tradition in conserving wetlands (and thus meadows) especially for birds: Silver Meadows Appeal (1979), Pulborough Brooks Appeal (1991).

Scottish National Heritage,

12 Hope Terrace,
Edinburgh,
EH9 2AS.
Tel: 031 447 4784
Concerned with the conservation of meadows in Scotland.

Wild Flower Society,

68 Outwoods Road,
Loughborough,
LE11 3LY.
Promotes the conservation of wild flowers.

USA

Mt Cuba Centre,
PO Box 3570
Barley Mill Road,
Greenville,
Delaware,
19807–0570.
Tel: 302 239 4244
The gardens are dedicated to the conservation of the wild plants of the Appalachian Piedmonts. The extensive informal gardens offer the chance to see native flora at their best.

National Wildflower Research Centre Clearinghouse,
2600 FM 973 North,
Austin,
TX 78725,
USA.
Provides packages of information on all aspects of meadow creation, regional addresses, suppliers, books.

Natural Areas of Association,
320 South Third Street,
Rochford,
IL 61104.
Publishes the quarterly *Natural Area Journal* which sometimes includes articles on wilderness and meadows.

The Nature Conservancy,
1815 North Lynn Street,
Arlington,
Virginia, 22209.
Tel: 703 841 5300
Manages the largest private system of nature sanctuaries in the world – including many meadows; has 1,200 preserves in 50 states and in Canada, representing 2.3 million hectares.

The Wilderness Society,
900 Seventeenth Street,
NW Washington, DC 20006–2596.
Publishes a quarterly magazine. Aims to protect nations' remaining ancient forests and all precious wilderness and wildlife.

Various

Hunters of Chester Ltd,
The Old Estate Office,
Oulton Park,
Tarporley,
Cheshire,
CW6 9BL.
Tel: 0829 21 644/684
Fax: 0829 21 526
Hunter rotary strip seeders and Rotamix seeders for good lowland conditions.

The Natural History Museum,
South Kensington,
London,
SW7 5BD.
Tel: 071 938 8955
'Meadows' wallchart, 60 cm x 78 cm.

Watkins & Doncaster,
Four Throws,
Hawkhurst,
Kent,
TN18 5ED.
Tel: 0580 753133
Demonstration cases for schools showing different seed dispersal mechanisms.

World Pasture
There is a mine of information on the state of 'pastures' worldwide in the

1992 Environmental Almanac compiled by the World Resources Institute (published by Houghton Mifflin, Boston). For instance, in the profiles for each of the states of the United States percentages of different types of habitat are given. Only three states have more than 20 per cent pastures – Kentucky (42 per cent), Missouri (30 per cent) and Tennessee (about 20 per cent). The following states have 10–20 per cent: Alabama, Arkansas, Florida, Hawaii, Iowa, Mississippi, New York, Oklahoma and Virginia. The remainder have significantly less than 10 per cent. As for the Canadian provinces, the mainland ones have significantly less than 5 per cent – almost nil – and Prince Edward Island has about 5 per cent pasture.

The Environmental Almanac also lists the main habitats found in different countries of the world. Those countries which have more 'pasture' than any other habitat (e.g. 'cropland', 'forest', 'other') include, in Africa, Botswana, Burkina Faso, Ethiopia, Lesotho, Madagascar, Morocco, Mozambique, Sierra Leone, Somalia, South Africa, Swaziland, Zambia, Namibia; in the Americas, Argentina, Costa Rica, Dominican Republic, Mexico, Nicaragua, Paraguay; in Europe, Greece, Ireland, Switzerland, United Kingdom; and elsewhere, Afghanistan, Australia, Mongolia, New Zealand and Syria.

GLOSSARY

Acarines – mites, i.e. tiny spiders, sometimes microscopic.

Acidic soil – soil water which has a pH of less than 6.5.

ADAS – Agricultural Development and Advisory Service.

Adventive – a non-native plant growing in a different habitat from its original habitat.

Aftermath – what is left on the ground after haymaking.

Alkaline soil – soil water which has a pH of more than 6.5.

Alluvial meadow – a meadow which is subjected to regular flooding during which silty deposits are left behind. *See* flood meadow, water meadow.

Alpine – any area above 1,000 metres in altitude.

Alpine meadow soil – soil above the tree-line, which has a small amount of leaf litter and duff.

Anodyne – a drug which alleviates pain.

AONB – Area of Outstanding Natural Beauty.

ASSI – Area of Special Scientific Interest (Northern Ireland only).

Beonet – Anglo-Saxon for a place covered in coarse grasses, thus 'Bent' in Bentley, etc.

Bog – a habitat with acid water on peat.

Butte – an isolated hill or peak.

Calcareous – soil or rock which is rich in calcium salts derived from chalk or limestone.

Calicole – a plant which prefers chalky soil.

Califuge – a plant which hates chalky soil.

Carrier – a man-made ditch used for flooding a water meadow.

Causse – French for a limestone plateau.

CFWR – Center for Wildflower Research (Texas).

Chaparral – a habitat which has long dry summers and cool, moist winters, resulting in grassy and scrubby expanses of vegetation.

Charismatic megafauna – one biologists marvel, the flora and fauna of the Arctic Wildlife Refuge in Alaska.

Colourscaping – an American

term for landscaping with colourful plants.

Cultivar – a variety of a plant produced and maintained by cultivation.

Diversity – the number of different species in a particular area, i.e. species-richness.

Duff – fibrous material resulting from decomposition.

Dune pasture – pasture which develops on mature dunes, or machair.

Dune slack – a low-lying area between mature sand dunes which has its own interesting flora and which is periodically flooded with sea water.

Endemic – native to, and restricted to, a particular geographical area.

ESA – Environmentally Sensitive Area.

étang – French for a shallow lake by the sea.

Eutrophic – conditions typical of eutrophication.

Eutrophication – the enrichment of ditches and waterways by agricultural chemicals which run off or leach from the soil, often causing a bloom of algae.

Exotic – a plant introduced from the East, such as Japan or China.

Extensification – reduction in farming intensification to once traditional methods.

Fen – a habitat in which peat overlies chalk.

Fennoscandia – a region which encompasses Norway, Sweden and Finland but excludes Denmark.

Flood meadow – a meadow which is flooded naturally by a stream or river. *See* alluvial meadow, water meadow.

Flora obsidionalis – siege flora.

Foggage – the growth of aftermath after haymaking.

Fold – to restrain sheep to a certain grazing or sleeping area using portable hurdles, thus folding sheep.

FWAG – Farming and Wildlife Advisory Group.

Gene pool – the total collection of genes and genetic material of a population of organisms.

Glean – to gather or pick a field after harvest for what is remaining; one who gleans is a 'gleaner'.

Glebe meadows – meadows belonging to the Church, sometimes cultivated.

Grinsard – Old English for roadside verges, a corruption of greensward.

Improved – a term used by farmers to mean draining the land (often damp meadows) and applying selective herbicides, or ploughing in order to grow crops such as ryegrass. In no way does it 'improve' the habitat in conservation terms, in fact the opposite.

Indicator – a plant or an animal which is indicative of a particular habitat, especially used in determining an ancient site.

Indigenous species – a native species which occurs in a specific locality.

Introduced species – a species which is introduced from one country to another where it is not native.

Lag, Lagg – a long narrow marshy meadow; an old Sussex term.

Landschaftsfresser – German for habitat destruction, literally 'landscape-eater', that might result from development.

Leaching – the process whereby chemicals disperse in solution through the soil to the nearest drainage ditch and thus to a stream, river and then the ocean. Leaching causes eutrophic pollution.

Limestone – a sedimentary rock which contains a large amount of calcium carbonate.

LFA – Less Favourable Area, i.e. one containing poor-grade soil, often in upland or mountainous areas.

Lomas – plains in south-western California.

Lusitanican – of southern origin.

Machair – a habitat type developed on wind-blown sand, often calcareous, undulating and subject to cultivation.

Marsh – a habitat in which peat occurs on rotting vegetation.

Meadsmen – men who worked in meadows.

Mesa – flat topped hill, wider than a butte, but smaller than a plateau.

Miniaturization – the effect of wind and sometimes sea spray on plants, which consequently grow in miniature form; very typical of coastal meadow plants.

Mire – a collective term for bogs and fens, in which the vegetation is rooted in wet peat.

Native species – or indigenous: species which occurs naturally in a given area.

Naturalized – the assimilation of an introduced species into a new environment, sometimes at the native species' expense.

NCC – Nature Conservancy Council, now English Nature, Countryside Council for Wales, Joint Nature Conservation Committee.

NERC – Natural Environment Research Council.

Neutral grasslands, or soils – areas in which the soil has a pH of 7, or neutral, neither acidic or alkaline.

Niche – the particular role of a plant or an animal in the environment.

NNR – National Nature Reserve; has higher status than SSSI.

Nutrient-poor soil – soil which is poor in nutrients.

Nutrient-rich soil – soil which is rich in nutrients.

Paigle Mead – old Kent name for a cowslip meadow.

pH – a measure of the hydrogen ions in solution, which gives an idea of the relative alkalinity or acidity of a soil or water sample.

Pingo – a unique type of grassy habitat formed during the last Ice Age by water coming to the surface and pushing an ice bell upwards.

Prairie – a French word meaning 'meadow-tract'.

Rare species – species with small populations that are not presently endangered or vulnerable, but which are at risk.

Re-create (of a meadow) – to establish a similar meadow as a typical one of the past.

Red Data Books – A series of books for most groups of plants and animals which catalogues the status of endangered and vulnerable species.

Reinstate (of a meadow) – to establish a replica meadow on the same site as a previously existing one.

RHS – Royal Horticultural Society.

Rogues – cornfield weeds.

Ruhezonen – German for an area which should be left undisturbed for nature conservation.

Seed bank – a collection of seeds of various species, sometimes economic ones, stored under artificial conditions below freezing and with a decreased water content to in-crease their longevity; or a natural seed bank which survives in the soil for a number of years or decades.

Semi-natural habitat – habitat which has been altered by management by man.

Set-aside – a system whereby agricultural land is taken out of production.

Shoddy – the term for waste wool from the wool industry, often with seeds adhering to it, which is discarded, sometimes in the countryside.

SSSI – Site of Special Scientific Interest.

Stamen – the male part of a flower which produces the male gametes, or pollen.

Stigma – the female part of a flower which receives the male pollen.

Sub-alpine – that area immediately below the tree-line.

Sward – a mixture of grasses and other wild plants.

Taiga – the boreal forests and its margins and clearings in northern latitudes; a part of the tundra.

Talkoo Work – a Finnish term for the communal gathering-in of the harvest.

Teart pastures – pastures which induce scouring in cattle, as a result of the presence of the trace element molybdenum.

Tree-line – the limit of tree growth, which varies according to different regions, but the coniferous tree-line is always slightly higher than the deciduous tree-line.

Tundra – treeless plain of the Arctic and Antarctic which has sedges, rushes and wood-rushes, as well as grasses.

Umbellifer – a member of the *Umbelliferae* family.

Unimproved – a term used to indicate meadow or other habitat which has not been adversely affected, or agriculturally improved, by man.

Urban colour – colour provided by plants in an urban environment.

Vulnerable species – species believed likely to move into the endangered category in the near future if the reasons for decline continue.

Water meadow – meadow which is artificially flooded by man, by various means.

Wilderness – an extensive habitat which has never been subjected to interference by man.

BIBLIOGRAPHY AND REFERENCES

Ajilvskgi, G., *Butterfly Gardening for the South, cultivating plants that attract butterflies*. Dallas, Taylor Publishing Company, 1991.

Allan, Mea, *E.A. Bowles and his garden at Myddelton 1865–1954*. London, Faber & Faber, 1973.

Allan, Mea, *William Robinson 1838–1935, Father of the English Flower Garden*. London, Faber & Faber, 1982.

Anderson, E., 'The rare and extraordinary plants of Presque Isle', *Pennsylvania*, August 1987, pp. 33–8.

Anonymous, *A Dictionary of Daily Wants*. London, Houlston & Wright, 1866.

Arden, H., 'John Muir's Wild America', *National Geographic*, April 1973, pp. 433–58.

Austin, Richard L., *Wild Gardening, strategies and procedures using native plantings*. New York, Fireside Books, Simon & Schuster Inc., 1985.

Baker, H., 'Alluvial meadows: A comprehensive study of grazed and mown meadows', *Journal of Ecology*, Vol. 25, 1937, pp. 408–20.

Beningfield, G., Pailthorpe, R. and Payne, S., *Barclay Wills' The Downland Shepherds*, Stroud, Alan Sutton, 1989.

Brandon, P., *The Sussex Landscape*. Sevenoaks, Hodder & Stoughton, 1974.

Breymeyer, A.I., *Managed Grasslands: Regional Studies of the Ecosystems of the World*, Vol. 17A The Distribution and Management of Grasslands in the British Isles and Vol. 17B Grasslands in Upland Areas: The Massif Central (France). Amsterdam, Elsevier, 1990.

Brian, A., ed., *The Lugg Meadows near Hereford*. Hereford Nature Trust, 1991.

Brown, D.E. and Carmony, N.B., *Aldo Leopold's Wilderness, selected early writings by the author of A Sand County Almanac*. Harrisburg, Stackpole Books, 1990.

Buckingham, Helen, *Monitoring Grassland Transport Sites. Bromton Meadow SSSI Phase III*. Peterborough, Nature Conservancy Council, November 1987.

Buckley, P., 'Vanishing Meadows', *Kent Wildlife Focus*, Autumn/Winter 1991, pp. 6–7.

Carter, C. and Anderson, M., *Enhancement of Forest Ridesides and Roadsides to benefit Wild Plants and Butterflies*. Wrecclesham, Forestry Commission Research Division, 1987.

Castri, di F., Hansen, A.J. and Debussche, M., *Biological Invasions in Europe and the Mediterranean Basin*. Monographie Biologicae 65, Dordrecht, Boston, London, Kluwer Academic Publications, 1990.

Center for Wildflower Research, *Wildflower Handbook*. Austin, Texas, 1990.

Chambers, John, *Wild Flower Gardening*. London, Women's Institute and Ward Lock, 1989.

Clapham, A.R., Tutin, T.G. and Warburg, E.F., *Flora of the British Isles*. Cambridge, Cambridge University Press, 1962.

Countryside Commission, *Countryside Stewardship: an outline*. Cheltenham, Countryside Commission, 1991.

Darwin, C., *The Formation of Vegetable Mould Through the Action of Earthworms*. London, Faber & Faber, 1974.

Davis, T., 'Open Space', *Buzzworm, The Environmental Journal*, Vol. 3, No. 4, July/August 1991, pp. 18–19.

Doherty, J., 'Water over the Meadows', *Natural World*, Winter/Summer 1985, pp. 17–19. Excellent review of the history of water meadows.

Dony, J.G., Jury, S.L. and Perring, F.H., *English Names of Wild Flowers*. Reading, Botanical Society of the British Isles, 1986.

Dowdeswell, W.H., *The Life of the Meadow Brown*. London, Heinemann Educational Books, 1981.

Drabble, P., *My Wilderness in Bloom*. London, Michael Joseph, 1986. See chapter 46, Fragrant Harvest.

Duffey, E., *Nature Reserves and Wildlife*. London, Heinemann Educational Books, 1974.

Duffey, E., 'Lowland Grasslands and Heaths', chapter in *The Natural History of Britain and Ireland*. London, Michael Joseph, 1981, pp. 95–133.

Eathorne, R., 'Fade to Black: The Untold Story in the ANWR Battle', *Buzzworm, The Environmental Journal*, Vol. 3, No. 4, July/August 1991, pp. 34–5.

Elliott, E. and P., 'Wildflowers of a Texan spring', *The Garden*, Vol. 109, No. 11, 1984, pp. 454–6.

Feltwell, John, 'Roadside verges as refuges for orchids; is verge-cutting good for the species?', *Orchid Review*, Vol. 89, No. 1054, 1981, pp. 245–7.

Feltwell, John, 'Butterfly Behaviour – *Celtis, Crataegi, Spini*, Notes and Observations', *Entomologist's Record and Journal of Variation*, Vol. 95, 1983, pp. 169–70.

Feltwell, John, *A Guide to Countryside Conservation*. London, Women's Institute and Ward Lock, 1988. See especially chapter 1: Meadows, pp. 8–22.

Feltwell, John, *The Naturalist's Garden*. London, Ebury Press, 1988; New York, Salem House, 1988.

Feltwell, J., 'Camargue reflections', *Countryside*, Autumn 1990, pp. 16–17.

Feltwell, J. and Philp, E., 'Natural History of the M20 Motorway', *Transactions of the Kent Field Club*, Vol. 8, No. 2, 1980, pp. 101–14.

Fendig, G. and Stewart, E., *Native Flora of the Golden Isles*. Savannah, Fendig & Stewart, 1970.

Ferguson, W.S., Lewis, A.H. and Watson, S.J., 'The Teart pastures of Somerset', *Journal of Agricultural Science*, Vol. 33, 1943, pp. 44–51.

Fielder, J., *Colorado, Images of the Alpine Landscape*. Englewood, Colorado, Westcliffe Publishers Inc., 1985.

Fisher, J., *Mr Marshal's Flower Album, from the Royal Library at Windsor Castle*. London, Victor Gollancz Limited, 1985.

Fraser, K., 'Profiles, fritillaries and hairy violets: Miriam Rothschild', *New Yorker*, 19 October, 1987.

Fream, W., 'On the Flora of Water-Meadows, with Notes in the Species', *Journal of the Linnean Society, Botany*, Vol. 24, pp. 454–64, 1887–8.

Fuller, R.M., 'The changing extent and conservation interest of lowland grasslands in England and Wales, A review of grassland surveys, 1930–84', *Biological Conservation*, Vol. 40, 1987, pp. 281–300.

Gardening from Which?, 'Creating a Mini-Meadow', *Gardening from Which?*, September/October 1991, pp. 331–3.

Gibbons, B., 'North Meadow, Cricklade, Wiltshire', *British Wildlife*, Vol. 1, No. 4, 1990, pp. 216–18.

Gifford, J. and Bellamy, D., *Wilderness Britain*. Oxford, Oxford Illustrated Press, 1991.

Gillespie, Annie Paulson, 'Home Meadows Confronting Weed Ordinances', *Wildflower*, Fall/Winter 1990, pp. 12–19.

Green, C.B. and Porter, A.J., *Grasslands, Hedges and Trees*. Sevenoaks, Arnold Wheaton, 1986.

Greig, J., 'Some evidence of the development of grassland plant communities', *Archaeology and the Flora of the British Isles*, Report of the Botanical Society of the British Isles meeting, 1988, pp. 39–54.

Grey-Wilson, C., *The Alpine Flowers of Britain and Europe*. London, Collins, 1979.

Grieve, M., *A Modern Herbal*. Harmondsworth, Penguin, 1980. Useful for old names of meadow plants.

Grigson, G., *Flowers of the Meadow*. London, King Penguin, 1950.

Grigson, G., *The Englishman's Flora*. London, Paladin, 1958.

Grime, J.P., 'Mechanisms promoting floristic diversity in calcareous grasslands', *Calcareous Grasslands – Ecology and Management*, Proceedings of a joint British Ecological Society/Nature Conservancy Council symposium, 14–16 September 1987 at the University of Sheffield, 1990, pp. 51–6.

Hare, T., *A Nature Conservation Strategy for London, London's Meadows and Pastures. (Neutral Grassland)*. Ecology Handbook 8, London, The London Ecology Unit, 1988.

Hazel, V., *Hampshire Countryside Heritage: Meadows*. Winchester, Hampshire County Council, 1984.

Holden, E., *The Country Diary of an Edwardian Lady*. Exeter, Webb & Bower Ltd, 1977.

Hopkins, J.J., 'British Meadows and Pastures', *British Wildlife*, Vol. 1, No. 4, 1990, pp. 202–15.

Horwood, A.R., *A New British Flora, British Wild Flowers in their natural haunts, Vol. ii, Fields and meadows, cornfields, sea-coast*. London, The Gresham Publishing Company, 1919.

Hubbard, C.E., *Grasses: a guide to their structure, identification, uses, and distribution in the British Isles*. Harmondsworth, Penguin, 1968.

Jefferies, Richard, *Wild Life in a Southern County*. London, Thomas Nelson, 1925.

Jefferies, Richard, *The Life of the Fields*. London, Chatto & Windus, 1884.

Jefferies, Richard, *The Open Air*. London, Chatto & Windus, 1885.

Johnson, Lady Bird, 'Texas in Bloom', *National Geographic*, Vol. 173, No. 4, April 1988, pp. 493–9.

Johnson, Lady Bird and Lees, Carlton B., *Wildflowers Across America*. New York, Abbeville Press, 1988.

Keane, Maryangela, *The Burren*. The Irish Heritage Series No. 30, Norwich, Jarrold & Sons Ltd, 1983.

Knight, J., 'Conserving the green-winged orchid at the Royal Aerospace Establishment, Farnborough', *Sanctuary*, No. 20, 1991, p. 34.

Lambrick, G. and Robinson, M., 'The development of floodplain grassland in the Upper Thames Valley', *Archaeology and the Flora of the British Isles*, Report of the Botanical Society of the British Isles meeting, 1988, pp. 55–75.

Langer, R.H.M., *Pastures: Their Ecology and Management*. Oxford, Oxford University Press, 1990.

Lawes, J.B., 'Agricultural, Botanical, and Chemical Results of Experiments on the Mixed herbage of Permanent Meadow, conducted for more than twenty years in succession on the same Land. – Part 11 The Botanical Results, *Philosophical Transactions*, Part IV, 1882.

Lees, D.R. and Steward, J.A., 'Localized industrial melanism in the spittlebug *Philaenus spumarius (L.) (Homoptera:Aphrophoridae)*, Cardiff docks, south Wales', *Biological Journal of the Linnean Society*, Vol. 31, 1987, pp. 333–45.

Leopold, A., *A Sand Country Almanac, with other essays on conservation from Round River*. New York, Oxford University Press, 1966.

Le Lièvre, Audrey, *Miss Willmott of Warley Place, her life and her gardens*. London and Boston, Faber & Faber, 1980.

Liberty Hyde Bailey Hortorium staff, *Hortus Third, A Concise Dictionary of Plants Cultivated in the United States and Canada*. London, Collier Macmillan; New York, Macmillan, 1976.

Lousley, J.E., *Wild Flowers of Chalk and Limestone*. New Naturalist Series No. 16, London and Glasgow, Collins, 1950.

McDonald, A., 'Changes in the flora of Port Meadow and Picksey Mead, Oxford', *Archaeology and the Flora of the British Isles*, Report of the Botanical Society of the British Isles meeting, 1988, pp. 76–86.

Marshall, A., 'Legacy of the Crusaders', *Botanical Society of the British Isles News*, September 1991, pp. 33–4.

Martin, Laura C., *The Wildflower Meadow Book: A Gardener's Guide*. Chester, Connecticut, The Globe Pequot Press, 1988.

Measures, D.G., *Bright Wings of Summer*. London, Cassell, 1976.

Molinier, R. and Vignes, P., *Ecologie et Biocenitique, les êtres vivants leur milieux, leur communautés, l'environment*. Paris, Delachaus et Niestle, 1971.

Moore, I., 'Pastures: not as good as they were?', *Country Life*, 5 July, 1973, pp. 52–4.

National Geographic Society, *Wilderness USA*. Washington DC, National Geographic Society, 1973. See especially 'Where Have All The Prairies Gone?'

Natural Environment Research Council, *Report of the Unit of Comparative Plant Ecology, 1988–90*. Sheffield, Natural Environment Research Council, 1990.

Nature Conservancy Council, *Conserving Old Grassland*. Peterborough, Nature Conservancy Council, 1979.

Nature Conservancy Council, *The Conservation of Coastal Cliffs and Scarps*. Peterborough, Nature Conservancy Council, 1982.

Nature Conservancy Council, *The Conservation of Sand Dunes*. Peterborough, Nature Conservancy Council, 1982.

Nature Conservancy Council, *North Meadow, Cricklade*. Peterborough, Nature Conservancy Council, 1988.

Nature Conservancy Council, *The Conservation of Cornfield Flowers*. Peterborough, Nature Conservancy Council, 1989.

Neuray, G., *Des Paysages, Pour Qui? Pourquoi? Comment?* Gembloux, Les Presses Agronomiques de Gembloux, 1982.

Ogilvie, John, *The Imperial Dictionary of The English Language: A Complete encyclopedic Lexicon, Literary, Scientific, and Technological.* London, Blackie & Son, 1888.

Page, R., *The Education of a Gardener.* Harmondsworth, Penguin, 1983.

Padilla, V., *Southern California Gardens, An Illustrated History.* Berkeley and Los Angeles, University of California Press, 1961.

Parsons, M.E., *The Wildflowers of California, their names, haunts, and habits.* New York, Dover, 1966.

Partsch, K. and Zaunberger, K., *Report: The Alps.* Sonthofen, Alpen–und Europaburö, 1991.

Perring, F.H. and Farrell, L., *British Red Data Books: No. 1, Vascular Plants,* 2nd edition. Lincoln, The Royal Society for Nature Conservation, 1983.

Peterken, G., *Wildlife Conservation and Management.* London and New York, Chapman & Hall, 1981.

Plantlife, *Death Knell for Bluebells? Global Warming and British Plants.* London, Natural History Museum: Plantlife, 1991.

Pollard, E., Hooper, M.D. and Moore, N.W., *Hedges.* New Naturalist Series No. 58, London, Collins, 1974.

Polunin, O., *The Concise Flowers of Europe.* Oxford, Oxford University Press, 1981.

Rackham, O., 'Wildwood', *Archaeology and the Flora of the British Isles,* Report of the Botanical Society of the British Isles meeting, 1988, pp. 3–6.

Ranwell, D. S., ed., *Sand Dune machair 2,* Natural Environment Research Council report on meeting at the University of Aberdeen 24–5 September 1975. Cambridge, Institute of Terrestrial Ecology, 1977.

Reisigl, Herbert and Keller, Richard, *Alpenpflanzen im Lebensraum, AlpineRosen Schutt-und Felsvegetation.* Stuttgart and New York, Gustav Fischer Verlag, 1987.

Ricou, G., *Recyclage des feces et faune associée dans les ecosystemes degrades: paturages d'altitude et garrigue.* L'université de Rennes, France, 1984.

Riviere, S., *La Vallée de la Renarde.* Cahors, Tardy Quercy, 1981.

Robinson, E. and Summerfield, G., *John Clare, The Shepherd's Calendar*. Oxford Paperback Series, London, Oxford and New York, Oxford University Press, 1964.

Robinson, W., *Wild Garden*. London, John Murray, 1870; London, Century Publishing Company, 1983. See particularly, 'Early Flowering Bulbs in Meadow Grass', pp. 16–22.

Robinson, W., *Alpine Flowers for English Gardens*. London, John Murray, 1879.

Rothschild, M., 'Roosting behaviour of the Orange Tip in a flowery meadow in Normandy, yet another instance of male chauvinism', *Antenna*, Vol. 6, No. 3, 1982, pp. 252–3.

Rothschild, M., 'Farming with Wild Flowers', *Country Landowner*, May 1984, pp. 24–6.

Rothschild, M., 'Changing conditions and conservation at Ashton Wold, the birthplace of the SPNC', *Biological Journal of the Linnean Society*, Vol. 32, 1987, pp. 161–70.

Rothschild, M., 'Ashton Wold, changes in flora and fauna between 1900–1989, *Natural History of Northamptonshire*, 1989, pp. 29–38.

Rothschild, M., 'Gardening with butterflies', *Butterfly Gardening: Creating summer magic in your Garden*, Xerces Society, 1990, pp. 7–15.

Rothschild, M. and Farrell, C., *The Butterfly Gardener*. London, Michael Joseph Rainbird, 1983.

Roudil, J.L. and Canet, H., *Cambous, Village Prehistorique*. Societe Languedocienne de Prehistoire Guide no. 1, Montpellier, Ministere de l'Environnement et du Conseil General de l'Hérault, 1982.

Royal Society for Nature Conservation, *Disappearing Wildflowers*. Lincoln, Royal Society for Nature Conservation, 1987.

Royal Society for Nature Conservation, *Losing Ground, Vanishing Meadows, the case for extending the ESA principle*. Lincoln, Royal Society for Nature Conservation, The Wildlife Trusts Partnership, 1991.

Sackville-West, V., *Garden Book*. London, Futura, 1968.

Sage, B., 'Alpine village in danger', *New Scientist*, 4 October 1979, pp. 30–1.

Salisbury, E., *Weeds and Aliens*. London, Collins, 1961.

Sargent, C., *Britain's Railway Vegetation*. Abbots Ripton, Huntingdon, Institute of Terrestrial Ecology, 1984.

Scheffel, R.L., ed., *Our National Parks, America's Spectacular Wilderness Heritage*. Pleasantville, New York and Montreal, Reader's Digest, 1985.

Schröter, L., *Taschenflora des Alpen-Wanderers*. Zurich, Albert Raustein, 1880.

Schröter, C., *Das Pflanzenleben der Alpen*. Zurich, Albert Raustein, 1904.

Scott, J.A., *The Butterflies of North America: a natural history and field guide*. Stanford, Stanford University Press, 1986.

Sheail, J., 'Formation and maintenance of water meadows in Hampshire', *Biological Conservation*, Vol. 2, 1971, pp. 101–6.

Sheail, J., *Nature in Trust, The History of Nature Conservation in Britain*. Glasgow and London, Blackie, 1976.

Shoard, M., *The Theft of the Countryside*. London, Maurice Temple Smith Ltd, 1980.

Smith, C.J., *Ecology of the English Chalk*. London, Academic Press, 1980.

Smith, R.S., *Conservation of Northern Uplands Meadows*. Bainbridge, Yorkshire Dales National Park Authority, 1985.

Smith, R.S., 'Farming and the conservation of traditional meadowland in the Pennine Dales Environmentally Sensitive Area', *Ecological Change in the Uplands*, British Ecological Society Special Publication No. 7, Blackwell Scientific Publications, 1988.

Smith, R.S. and Jones, L., 'The phenology of mesotrophic grassland in the Pennine Dales, Northern England: Historic hay cutting dates, vegetation variation and plant species phenologies', *Journal of Applied Ecology*, Vol. 28, 1991, pp. 42–59.

'Reserves in Trust', *Natural World*, Winter 1982, p. 13.

Streeter, D., 'Natural Grasslands', *Natural World*, Winter 1985, pp. 28–9.

Thacker, C., *The History of Gardens.* Berkeley and Los Angeles, University of California Press, 1985.

Thomas, E., *Richard Jefferies.* London and Boston, Faber & Faber, 1978.

Thompson, Flora, *Lark Rise to Candleford.* London, Penguin Master Classics, 1977.

Thoreau, Henry David, *Cape Cod.* London, Penguin, 1987.

Timme, S.L., *Wild Flowers of Mississippi.* Jackson, Mississippi, University of Mississippi Press, 1989.

Tosco, U., *Mountain Flowers.* London, Orbis Publishing Limited, 1974.

Vines, Gail, 'Science can make a meadow', *New Scientist*, 18 August 1983, p. 486.

Waring, P., 'The moths of Bernwood meadows – a brief review based on work from 1984–86', *Oxfordshire Invertebrate Group Newsletter*, Vol. 1, 1988, pp. 10–17.

Waring, P., 'Observations on invertebrates collected up during wild flower seed harvesting in a hay meadow, with particular reference to the butterflies and moths', *British Journal of Entomology and Natural History*, Vol. 3, 1990, pp. 143–52.

Weathers, L.A., 'Flowers wild and wonderful', *Southern Living*, April 1990, pp. 90–5.

Wells, D.A. and Oswald, P.H., *The Conservation of Meadows and Pastures.* Northampton, Nature Conservancy Council, 1988.

Wells, T., Bell, S. and Frost, A., *Creating attractive grasslands using native plant species.* Peterborough, Nature Conservancy Council, 1981.

Williams, L.R., 'Hay meadow flora at Fryent Country Park, Middlesex', *London Naturalist*, Vol. 65, 1986, pp. 65–81.

Williams, L.R., *Fryent Country Park Hay Meadow Survey Reports 1986.* London, London Borough of Brent, 1988.

World Resources Institute, *The 1992 Information Please Environmental Almanac.* Boston, Houghton Mifflin, 1991.

INDEX